The School for Scandal

THEATRE CLASSICS FOR THE MODERN READER

To reproduce the values and effects of the theatre on the printed page is the ambitious aim of this series of the classics of the stage. Although good plays have always been read as well as acted, few playwrights before the era of Ibsen and Shaw have ever written with any public other than the theatre audience sharply in their minds. In consequence, the reader of older plays is usually required to supply his own visualizing of the staging and his own interpretation of stage action and even the manner of the delivery of the lines themselves. Frequently he is also required to put up with abbreviations and other space-saving printing devices.

This modern reader's edition of theatre classics vitalizes the outstanding plays of the past with the kind of eye-pleasing text and the kinds of reading and acting guides to which today's reader is accustomed in good published editions of twentieth century dramas. The text itself has not been altered except for occasional modernizations of spelling and punctuation (common to all modern editions of earlier works) and the rare use of italics for emphasis when the reading of a line is not immediately clear. Essentially, that is, the author's text is as he wrote it. Added to it are descriptions of scenes and costumes, indications of expression and action, and explanation of words and references not readily comprehensible.

The illustrations should aid immeasurably in visualizing the play. A description of the original staging, stage conditions, and stage techniques is provided partly as still another aid to visualization but principally to show how the playwright adapted his materials to suit the particular stage conventions of his time. Companioning each play are also a sketch of the author's life, an analysis of the play, and a selective bibliography to make this as much an all-in-one edition as possible.

RICHARD BRINSLEY SHERIDAN

The School for Scandal

EDITED BY

VINCENT F. HOPPER and
GERALD B. LAHEY

New York University

WITH A NOTE ON THE STAGING

GEORGE L. HERSEY

Bucknell University

ILLUSTRATIONS BY

FRITZ KREDEL

BARRON'S EDUCATIONAL SERIES

Woodbury, New York

The School for Scandal

THE PLAYWRIGHT

From a literary standpoint, it is difficult to determine what should be said of Sheridan's life: for of his four careers (that of playwright, that of manager and part-owner of the Theatre Royal, Drury Lane, London, that of Parliamentary Member for Stafford and prominent Whig, and simultaneously a scintillating career as man of fashion and intimate friend of the First Gentleman of Europe) the first was over when Brinsley was little more than twenty-five. The others had hardly begun.

If Sheridan had died at the age of thirty, we should have mourned in him the premature loss of great fertility of wit and facility of invention and speculated on what he might have done had he lived to become an ancient like Shaw. The grief would have been vain: after his brilliant wooing of the comic muse, Sheridan immediately and almost completely abandoned her for other blandishments. For if Sheridan had died at the fall of the curtain on his highly successful burlesque *The Critic* in October of 1779, his literary reputation would stand just where it is.

Actually it was his dazzling, early conquest of the comic stage that enabled Sheridan to get control of the Drury Lane theatre; and it was the control of the theatre that enabled him to pay for the expensive election contests that made him a member of the House of Commons and the valued friend of the ravishing Duchess of Devonshire, Lady Bessborough, Mrs. Crewe, etc. As Whig politician and man of fashion, he bears some resemblance to his own Charles Surface: a man of endless gaiety, wit, and charm,—and debts. Like Oscar Wilde, all who met him found him one of his own best "productions." And like Surface, his gaiety flared up most brightly in adversity: we have the stories of his having to rent for an evening's entertainment of friends his own plate and china from the pawnbroker in whose more or less permanent custody it was. His theatre burned down in 1809 and was rebuilt again more imposingly despite lack of insurance. On the night of the fire, the ominous glare was visible through the windows of the House of Commons where Sheridan was scheduled to speak. On learning that his own theatre was in flames, he went to a neighboring tavern and, calmly ordering his drink, inquired whether a man might not have his glass of wine at his own fireside.

As for the Sheridan family history, it is as full of caprice and paradox as his career. In a sense he came naturally by his literary and stage interests: his mother Frances Sheridan was a moderately successful writer of novels and plays. Sheridan's celebrated Mrs. Malaprop was faintly anticipated in the character of Mrs. Tryfort in his mother's comedy *Journey to Bath*. His father, Tom Sheridan, an actor, had a limited success as theatre-manager in Smock Alley, Dublin. Later he was a fairly successful teacher of elocution in England. Richard Brinsley's grandfather, another Tom, a schoolmaster and scholar, was a friend of the great Swift. Hence Sheridan's verbal dexterity would seem naturally come by. However, the family history does not record progenitors remarkable for graceful and lively wit. Indeed the clerical grandfather lost a preferment by a particularly inept sermon delivered on the anniversary of the Hannoverian succession on the text "Sufficient unto the day is the evil thereof." Dr. Johnson, the literary dictator of his day, had said of Sheridan's father that he was "dull, naturally dull; but it must have taken him a great deal of pains to become what we now see him; such an excess of stupidity, Sir, is not in nature."

Regardless, in no part of Sheridan's life or personality does one find dullness. His life reads almost like the script of an over romantic musical comedy or light opera. Before he was twenty-one, he had participated in two duels and managed a romantic elopement to France with Miss Elizabeth Ann Linley; before he was thirty he had written two of the liveliest comedies in English, one of the best farces, and one of the best light operas. For over a quarter of a century he was one of the most brilliant figures in a Parliament that contained Pitt, Fox, and Burke. And his speech against Warren Hastings, lasting over five and a half hours and delivered with rapid stacatto brilliance without notes, achieved a reputation almost mythical in grandeur; it was regarded by competent members of the Parliament as exceeding in magnificence any comparable utterance in history. Even in the declining days of a life well saturated with port and claret, brandy and water, he could hold the critical Lord Byron spellbound by his conversation from six in the evening until midnight had passed. And even in his last days of poverty and penury, even then he was colorful in the squalor of his fall, with the officers of the law ready to carry his expiring frame to the debtor's den for debts. Johnson must have been right: the father's dullness must have been an acquired and hence not a transmittible trait: Brinsley inherited none of it.

Like his own sprightly Charles Surface, Sheridan managed to combine gallantry, gaiety, and gambling. His personal attractiveness enabled him to win the affections of Miss Linley, a beautiful and gifted daughter of a family that was apparently designed by Thomas Mann, so evident in it was the affinity of disease and precocious musical talent. All of the many children of the family were personally endowed with rare musical talent and personal beauty and were particularly susceptible to tuberculosis. The exquisite voice and fragile beauty of Sheridan's wife early succumbed to the tuberculary scourge. Sheridan then married in his forties a slip of a young thing, Hester Jane Ogle, barely twenty and daughter of a Dean of Westminster; it was she who remained devoted and faithful to Sherry despite his own amorous driftings, sharing with him at the end illness and misery. At that point, Sheridan was his own Charles Surface in reverse, all his personal effects being sold to stave off creditors so that he might stiffen at last in a rented room.

Sheridan was born in that cradle of writers of English comedy—Dublin, birthplace of Wilde and Shaw likewise. His life describes a brilliant arc rising from the poverty of 12 Dorset Street, Dublin, and passing like a meteor across the London horizon to sink into the poverty of 14 Savile Row; he was born in October of 1751 and died in July of 1816. It was a half century of events that shook mankind, and Sheridan was everywhere in touch with his time. Yet, in spite of Sheridan's brilliant personal success during the full tide of his career, the eighteenth century was aristocratic, and Sheridan's imposing friends always spoke of him as of low or humble origin. Walpole, for example, spoke of him as "the son of an Irish player," and his official biographer and countryman, Tom Moore, speaks of his "disadvantages of birth and station." Watkins, the memorialist, refers to him as one having neither "pedigree nor property." Actually, the Sheridans were gentry, of good family, with bishops and royal secretaries in the family history. But their gentility was somewhat legendary by 1751, and however good a defense of it by Sheridan's mother Frances in her *Memoir,* unless family bestowed privilege and property, rank and connection, it was of merely sentimental value; Sheridan's family gave him only intelligence and vigor to which he added great charm of manner.

More need not be said of Sheridan's family than that poverty drove them to England; from England they took refuge temporarily in France from importunate creditors, leaving Richard Brinsley, however, to be educated at Harrow. Despite the fact that two of the plays of Sheridan's mother were produced by Garrick at Drury Lane in 1763, debts drove the family cross channel to France in 1764. Richard had been entered at Harrow in 1762, the Sheridans being acquainted with Dr. Sumner, the headmaster of the famous foundation. Biographers in general agree in saying that he was unhappy there (he stayed for about six years) at a most impressionable period of a young boy's life. He was evidently made conscious of the fact that he was the son of a poor player who had already strutted and fretted his hour upon the stage; he often felt depressed and dispirited, insignificant and neglected; the experience left him perhaps with a permanent sense of insecurity and social inadequacy, of sensitivity to status. Thirty-five years after he had left Harrow, he still recalled the place with gloom. Lady Holland (and some others), who rather specialized in the slightly malicious detection of the weaknesses of others, gave it as her opinion that Sheridan's desire to rise in the world of politics, to become a great Parliamentary orator and political figure, was owing to a desire to compensate for the humbleness of his origins; his experience at Harrow lends some basis to support the view. Lady Holland also offered it as her view that his desire to take his place in the world of literature and fashion (as an intimate of the Prince Regent, for example), his gallantries, his infidelities to his two wives, was mainly owing to a vanity which was compensating for a sense of deficient pedigree in the great world of Whig fashion and magnificence.

He rejoined his family at Bath on their return from France in 1770. Whatever the psychic scars he bore away with him from Harrow, he did become a middling student of the classics although contemporaries felt him slightly undereducated by gentlemanly standards; that is to say, he substituted brilliance and vivacity for sobriety and gravity. Moreover, he did acquire a taste for reading and literary style; despite his own great oratorical success, he was better at Horace and Virgil than Demosthenes; he knew much of the poet Spenser and thoroughly admired Dryden. Indeed his own precarious hold on scholarship may have sharpened his wit and imagination for the conception of such figures as Mrs. Malaprop. Moore, his official biographer, tells us that Sheridan was never quite sure of his spelling, when to double his consonants, for example. Perhaps the phonetic vagaries of Mrs. Malaprop have their counterpart in the orthographic ones of her creator. Whatever his scholarly success at Harrow, the acquired prima donna temperament, the touchy sense of pride is important to his biographers. (Is Faulkland of *The Rivals* an externalization of this sensitive edge of his temper?) For if, as Lady Holland avers, it launched Sheridan into the sunny waters of comic drama, it also led him to abandon the craft. Rapidly successful at literary comedy (all of his brilliant comedy appeared between 1775 and 1780), Sheridan was determined to establish himself in the world of politics and fashion. For Sheridan realized that although England's aristocrats allowed artists to associate freely with them, this privilege was never to be mistaken for an acceptance as equals. And such was Brinsley's pride that an equal or the "role" of an equal would alone satisfy him.

After a political career of over thirty years, Sheridan told Creevey in 1805 that the happiest day of his life was that on which he was first elected to Parliament as the Member for Stafford. The romantic Shelley wrote (apparently with pride) that great authors, poets in particular, were the "unacknowledged legislators" of mankind. Sheridan, for all of his capricious, irresponsible, quixotic temper, was an eighteenth century man, not a romantic; he fully intended to achieve status by becoming one of the publicly acknowledged legislators of mankind, a situation which would allow him to move in the fashionable and fabulous Whig world with something like equal dignity. Hence he used his early literary success to acquire control of the policy and property of the Drury Lane theatre so that with the proceeds and profits of this venture he could pay his heavy election costs and fulfill his social duties. For about thirty years the theatre was to support the aspirations and activities, political and social, of Sheridan. It was mainly in connection with this theatre and its financing, reading its manuscripts, paying its actors, that Sheridan acquired his notorious reputation for procrastination and irregularity, for picturesque undependability. However, the business enabled him to remain a prominent Foxite

Whig for more than a quarter of a century, always a vigorous member of the Opposition. Perhaps then, as Lady Holland suggested, it was his sensitive pride that led him to seek a more elevated status and become one (to paraphrase Goldsmith on Burke)

Who, born for the theatre, at too early an age

To Party gave up what was meant for the stage.

We today cannot help thinking that there is more of interest in his literary comedies than in his Parliamentary utterances, which have indeed something of the theatrical, meretricious-sublime about them. Especially when Sheridan was seeking solemn elevation of sentiment, his oratory reads a little like the artificial flights of a Surface; Sheridan was, however, at his best in Parliament when the occasion required satiric ridicule and witty exposure of fraud and falseness. Then his oratory has the authentic literary ring about it. But although *meretricious* may possibly apply to his quality of utterance at moments, it never touched the quality of his motives. During this period when everywhere in Europe and England aspirations were awakening for independence and a higher status for the common man, Sheridan's pride forebade his taking up with the increasingly numerous Tory reactionary personalities and the rewards therefrom. Burke, for example, did not scruple to get cash and sinecure from his titled masters; Sheridan scrupulously avoided even the shadow of a suspicion of being for sale, even in those easy days. Neither a place nor a pension seeker, he always had about him the quixotic gesture of one who wore the poor-but-proud panache.

Perhaps a few more details about Sheridan, especially about his domestic and business personality, will suffice before considering the qualities of our particular play. His first wife was Elizabeth Ann Linley, the Bath nightingale, whose ethereal beauty and exquisite voice charmed everyone in England from the royal couple to the average chairman. She was the object of the flattering attentions, of the obsessions of men of all ages and ranks. She had already made the conquest of one rich middle-aged man, Walter Long, by the time she was sixteen. Already by 1771 a play, *The Maid of Bath,* had been written about her and the obsessive attachments which she inspired. Hence she had fame and unwelcome notoriety before she was twenty. She so captivated another elderly admirer that his oppressive attentions led to her elopement to France with Richard Brinsley Sheridan as her chivalrous protector. Parental intervention at length led to their return, and eventually they were wed for a second time, there being some doubt as to the validity of their French marriage. Sheridan's gallantry during this harassed period of Eliza's life, his chivalrous defense of her against Captain Mathews' offensive aggressiveness involved him early in two very fierce duels and gave him some practical insight into the Acres-O'Trigger scenes of *The Rivals.* And his conduct won for him forever the toast of the beaux, Miss Linley. In 1773, Elizabeth wrote to Brinsley that it was "not your person that gained my affection. No, Sheridan, it was that delicacy, that tender compassion . . . which induced me to love you." There was something of a rarefied Miss Lydia Languish in Elizabeth.

It was on April 13, 1773 that they were married for the second time at Marylebone church in London. When two days later the *Morning Post* announced that "Mr. Sheridan, a student of the Temple, is at last firmly united to the Maid of Bath, on Tuesday last," it was optimistic in the use of the adverb "firmly." Sheridan did not have a domestic temperament; he found it difficult to "settle down," but we are glad to believe with Lady Holland that his amorous digressions were products of social vanity, not personal vice. Even Eliza's deep devotion was at length weakened; in 1790 they were temporarily estranged by his inconstancies. Mrs. Sheridan had for a moment Candida's temptation; she said later of this period that had the royal Duke of Clarence been ten years older than he was, she might have yielded to his importunities to run away with him.

Again biographers have hinted that her daughter was the child of Lord Edward Fitzgerald, a result of a liaison contracted during despondency at her Sherry's waywardness. Perhaps this is one of the publications of the Scandal Club. At any rate, on her death, Sheridan realizing his own primary culpability could assert only that she was an angel. Indeed, Maria's devoted, faithful patience in waiting for Charles Surface's reform has in it a hint of Eliza's plight.

But Sheridan's life was not as sentimental as his comedy. Within three years of her death, Sheridan had married again; in his second marriage he assumed the role which he had ridiculed in Sir Peter Teazle, his bride, a buoyant twenty, and Brinsley a bottle-worn forty-three. However, he was still the incorrigible husband despite a complexion now ablaze with the consequences of steady drinking; the heart still wandered, and his Hester Jane Ogle—Mrs. Sheridan II—shared her husband with other beauties who wandered through the lustrous chambers of Devonshire, Burlington, or Carleton Houses. The second wife, daughter of the Dean of Winchester, perhaps offered Sherry in social position, and hence security, what the first wife offered in beauty and talent.

From the standpoint of his career, 1775 was the marvellous year in Sheridan's life. At the beginning of it, he was known only as the young husband of the beautiful Eliza; at the end, he was being celebrated as the writer of two of the best comedies in the English language. In 1774, he had written to his father that he was at work on a comedy for Mr. Harris of Covent Garden Theatre. It was produced as *The Rivals* in January of 1775. Not immediately successful, it was withdrawn from the stage and subjected to serious revision. Unlike Shaw, who in his day determined to re-educate his audience, Sheridan conformed quietly to the taste of his house, carefully observing the criticisms levelled against his original text and purging it of heaviness. The eleven days of his revision were among the most important of his life. The revised play was immediately popular and the hit of the season; Sheridan's name quickly became a token of brilliance. In November of the same year, Harrison produced for him *The Duenna,* a repository (economically enough) of many of the verses he had written for Eliza during his courtship; it was a sort of light opera, dialogue interspersed with songs, the music composed by his father-in-law Linley. It was also a triumph. In record for continuous performance it outdistanced the famed *Beggar's Opera*: forty years later Lord Byron still could not praise it too highly. The song-books made from it were as profitable as the theatrical presentation. Sheridan had had two great successes within a twelve month period.

As a result, the young husband now had enough money to support his wife and family. Actually, Eliza was quite willing to continue her highly lucrative career as a public singer. But Sheridan's quixotic pride forbade. Many people at the time felt that for a woman to expose herself to the public gaze was to diminish the glow of her maiden modesty; stage and screen celebrities have since learned to control this girlish shyness. But Sheridan wished that his wife should never appear as a paid public entertainer. And the success, the two successes of the year, made his wish practicable. With the enormous popularity of both productions, Sheridan found himself at little more than twenty-four a man who had arrived. Even Dr. Johnson (finding him in no sense as dull as the father) was moved to sponsor him for membership in the famed Literary Club, remarking, "He who has written the two best comedies of his age is surely a considerable man." Among the members were Gibbon, Burke, Fox. It was with Fox that Sheridan was to connect his political fortunes and future; perhaps the Literary Club was the original staging ground of his political career.

At any rate, Sheridan's success as a playwright enabled him to turn both socially and economically to grander enterprise. Between 1776 and 1778, succeeding to the great Garrick, Sheridan acquired control of the property and policy of the Drury Lane theatre. His financial manipulations in acquiring the structure and its patent defy the analysis of either contemporaries or historians. Obviously the prodigal and practically impecunious Sheridan had a knack for finance as elusive and complicated as that of Joseph Surface for moral and social situations. From this point on, his economic life crawled through an underground labyrinth of mortgages, borrowings, interest, credit, profits, payments that would have utterly baffled the simple gossips of the Scandal Club. It was Byron's opinion that Sheridan had handled everybody's money but his own. As a business man his name became a symbol for procrastination, irregularity; but his tactfulness and charm, his ingenuity and improvisation expanded to cover his impracticality, and for more than a quarter of a century, the Drury Lane theatre continued to support Sheridan's adventures into the fashionable life of London. Of course, it should be added that as Member of Parliament he was immune to arrest for debt. When after more than a quarter of a century in the House of Commons, he finally lost his seat, he was promptly in real difficulties for his endless arrears.

But unlike his own Charles Surface, Sheridan was not ultimately rescued from misfortunes and reckless prodigality of spending by a benevolent uncle returning from India. Rather, as his days drew to a close, his portraits by Gainsborough and Reynolds (even the noted one in which his wife represented St. Cecelia) were auctioned to pay part of his debts; finally the bailiff and sheriff were waiting to pick up the sick, broken man in bed and blanket to carry him off to the sponging house for indebtedness. Lord Byron's spoken epitaph for that forlorn figure was "poor dear Sherry, what a wreck is that man!" Ironically, despite the shabbiness and neediness of his last days, Sheridan was laid to rest in the poets' corner in Westminster Abbey; the poor player's son had as honorary pall-bearers royal dukes, earls, bishops, lords.

Sheridan is well summed up in a contemporary review of Tom Moore's *Memoirs of Sheridan*: "He . . . was for thirty years the most brilliant talker—the greatest conversational wit of the splendid circle in which he moved . . . Sheridan's conceptions . . . seem always to have flowed from him with great copiousness and rapidity. But he had taste as well as genius—and ambition as well as facility, . . . his labour . . . not in making what was bad tolerable, but in making what was good, better and best."

THE PLAY

The plot of the *School for Scandal* contains three obvious strands of which the titular component is really only a relatively small part: 1) the activities of the scandal club itself, 2) the mésalliance between the youthful country maid and the elderly, rich city man, and 3) the contest of the rival brothers for the hand of the sweet artless heiress, a contest between the "natural" man of free, generous-hearted, open disposition, and the "artificial" man of cool, close, contriving temper.

In a society so closely governed by tradition and custom as that of Sheridan's day, we need not be surprised that none of these separate plot-components, held rather loosely together by the rival-brothers motif, is altogether original. Obviously the scandal club reminds us of the "cabal nights" of Congreve's *Way of the World,* in which a select coterie of fashionable ladies and their foppish attendants "come together like the coroner's inquest to sit upon the murdered reputations of the week." Again, the honest but crusty old bachelor newly married to the eager, rustic country lass reminds us of Wycherly's *Country Wife*. Finally, all readers of Fielding's popular *Tom Jones* cannot fail to recall that Fielding, himself a dramatist turned novelist, had presented at length with appropriate "intrigue" the fortunes of the rival brothers (actually half-brothers in his story). So considerable is the resemblance between Sheridan and Fielding in the use of this motif that to discuss this aspect of the plot of *Tom Jones* is really a satisfactory way to summarize a part of the characterization and intrigue of the *School for Scandal*.

The Charles Joseph Surface contrast appears in *Tom Jones* as the Tom Jones-Young Blifil rivalry. Young Blifil is the type of the discreet, prudent, artful hypocrite whose glossy tactic of simulated virtue and pretense in-gratiates him with those in authority and influence about him, whereas Tom Jones is the type of the handsome, impulsive, generous-hearted young blood whose seeming irresponsibility and irregularities make him the scandal and despair of sober authority. For in spite of his open-hearted chivalrous disposition, his impulsive temperament involves him in a malodorous reputation for extravagant conduct in regard to women and drink. Conversely, Young Blifil's calculating artfulness enables him to turn occasion and circumstance against the "natural" man Tom Jones. Consequently, Tom becomes the scandal of Squire Allworthy as Charles becomes the scandal of Sir Peter Teazle. And as Young Blifil slyly insinuates himself into the graces of Squire Allworthy, so does Joseph Surface win the high regard of Sir Peter. In *Tom Jones,* as a result of this situation, Tom seems in a way to lose the hand of the beautiful, loving heiress (Sophia) much as is Charles in danger of alienating the regard of Maria. In both instances it is the case of the handsome young rake-hell who is to be finally reclaimed by the patient purity of womanly innocence. And just as the passionless Young Blifil schemes to win the hand of Sophia, who finds him totally unsatisfactory, so does Joseph endeavor to compass the person and fortune of Maria. Both men are interested in the fortune, not the person or character of the lady.

As the readers of *Tom Jones* know, Tom's redemption from imminent misery is finally brought about as a result of his benevolent and generous-hearted acts which have turned people and events in his favor when he is at the bottom of his fortunes. Likewise, under the smooth guidance of poetic justice, the hypocritical maneuverings of Young Blifil are exposed with the result that Sophia is to make a contented husband of the reformed rake and Tom is restored to fortune and the good graces of Squire Allworthy. We note that Charles Surface, Uncle Oliver, and Maria are brought together in much the same emotional context whereas Joseph Surface (the counterpart of Young Blifil) is left naked to laughter and cold winds.

Charles Surface, like Tom Jones, is the amatory center of the situation: the ladies hanker for both as handsome, dashing young men nicely spiced with rakishness. In particular, each has among his admirers a fashionable and mature lady of ripe and ready charms, and in both cases their affections are so strong as to lead to questionable tactics to gain their erotic objects: Tom has his Lady Bellaston; Charles, his Lady Sneerwell; both women are properly classified as *femmes dangereuses* (the descriptive categorization in the dramatis personae of the eighteenth century French translation *L'école du scandale*: it conveys the contemporary French view of Lady Sneerwell, as does *dissipateur* for Charles and *tartuffe* for Joseph). In both situations the disingenuous ladies are disappointed.

Descending to further particulars, there is in the *School for Scandal* the celebrated screen scene in which the supposed little French milliner is brilliantly disclosed at length as the little English coquette Lady Teazle. Perhaps the germ of this scene is also to be found in the clever concealment scene in *Tom Jones,* which is also a result of an illicit visit during which circumstances are complicated by the unexpected arrival of the one person least desired by the first caller; hence the need for hasty concealment of the first caller and the ensuing embarrassing dialogue. In *Tom Jones* Lady Bellaston makes a clandestine call at Tom's London lodgings in quest of an assignation; no sooner has she arrived than Mrs. Honour (the personal maid of the beloved Sophia) arrives. That Sophia should learn of Lady Bellaston's presence in his private chambers would be especially prejudicial to Tom's hopes for her; hence Lady Bellaston in concealment behind a curtain is the embarrassed listener to a conversation especially uncomplimentary to her. Tom meanwhile is desperately engaged in controlling the conversation, trying to dominate other aspects of the situation, and at the same time attempting to get rid of Mrs. Honour without further embarrassment and before detection. In this latter point he succeeds, unlike Joseph in the comparable situation. Of course, it is obvious that the device of the concealment is used extensively in Elizabethan comedy, as readers of *Volpone,* for instance, recall.

This comparison with *Tom Jones* has been made not so much as a comment on possible "sources" or to point out another of the traditional elements in Sheridan's play as to illuminate the particular quality of his genius. For if one aspect of genius is the capacity to take a hint, we can see how readily Sheridan improved upon the parallel elements we have noted in Fielding's novel. The screen scene, for instance. Sheridan has brilliantly expanded upon the situation, for whereas we barely recall Fielding's scene after a reading, Sheridan's improvisation is one of the most memorable in English drama—perhaps not less well known and delighted in than the balcony scene in *Romeo and Juliet.* And so effectively did Sheridan utilize his situation—the eventual emergence from concealment of the person *not* expected by those on the stage—that we find a century later Oscar Wilde borrows the idea for his *Lady Windermere's Fan.* As Lady Teazle is saved from the pit at the end of the path of dalliance by a sudden act of selfless generosity (Sir Peter's declaration of his intentions in regard to her), so is Lady Windermere saved by the sudden, self-effacing generosity of Mrs. Erlynne.

But neither Fielding nor Wilde possessed Sheridan's peculiar grace—that of lavishness: he gets his effects by elaborating as fully as possible on his given situation or character. For Sheridan, unlike Fielding in *Tom Jones* or Jonson in *Volpone,* is not satisfied with just one untimely and especially undesirable caller; they come not as single spies but in battalions: one, then another, then *another* like tight-rope walkers mounting one upon another's shoulders until the whole swaying structure collapses like the crack of a whip. If Sheridan were using as his given or inherited scene that of a discreet garden-party, he would transform it to a colorful and hilarious street carnival. In his art as well as in his life, he was a creature of coloratura effects and gay-hearted extravaganza.

In Fielding's Young Blifil, Sheridan might have seen the artful hypocrite angling for the fortune of one young lady; but Joseph Surface must have ambiguous involvements with at least three. Again, if the notion of a school for scandal, its fashionable ladies and fluttering fops, comes from Congreve, his people are amateurs. With Sheridan the amateur gathering becomes a formidable, established institution, with critical consciousness of styles of defamation much as though it were a sophisticated academy of painting and sculpture. We have had hypocrites before Joseph Surface; but when did one attempt to so weave the web of sophistry as to prove to a young wife that she had a canonical duty to cuckold the elderly husband. Uncles before have been kind to erring nephews, but when was there another Uncle Oliver who gave so much for so little? Whether we are auctioning off the family portraits or concealing the forbidden sweets of the circulating library (as in *The Rivals*), nothing will satisfy but a brilliant excess. In 1773, Goldsmith had given us a taste of the "man of sentiment" in Young Marlow; but whereas he had but one or two scenes of elevated flummery, Joseph's silky, false, smoothness of utterance envelops the entire play like a radiant bubble-bath. If Sir Oliver is to impersonate, it must be at least two people, and that in rapid succession. In his gay and dazzling elaboration of character and situation, Sheridan seems to feel about comedy what in his subsequent life he felt about the bottle, the boudoir, the parliamentary debate, about debts: only in glorious redundance is there sufficiency.

We have just made reference to Young Marlow of *She Stoops to Conquer* and Joseph Surface as satiric portrayals of the "man of sentiment." In regard to this point, our present comedy (like Goldsmith's) is something of a paradox. For although it ridicules the man of sentiment, it is itself, like its predecessor, a fulsome

specimen of sentimental comedy, Sheridan being unconsciously lavish in this latter characteristic.

The point is evident if we compare the *School for
Scandal* with Congreve's *Way of the World* (1700) or
with Fielding's handling of the prototypes of Charles
and Joseph. In regard to the former, we may note the
vast difference between Congreve's Millamant and Sheridan's Maria as types of the "heroine." The former is a
figure of brilliant, sophisticated, worldly poise, the latter
one of innocent, sweet, and artless simplicity. The elegant
Millamant is herself an active member of the "cabal
nights" or scandal gatherings who frankly relishes her
opportunities. Maria, however, primly abhors all wit and
satire which reflect maliciously upon human weaknesses.
Millamant glows with the lustrous cool radiance of the
crystal chandelier as she presides over her fashionable,
urbane gatherings. Maria is a cozy, comforting night-
light, a pleasantly dim domestic fixture. Such was the
shift in the type of sensibility admired in the heroine—
from transfigured worldly sense to shy, scrupulous sensitivity.

Further, if we compare specimens of the designing
lady, the *femme dangereuse,* in the two plays, we note
in Mrs. Marwood and Mrs. Fainall of Congreve's *Way
of the World* a ruthlessness and amorality only dimly
shadowed forth in Lady Sneerwell; and as for the flirta-
tious Lady Teazle, she seems inwardly blessed with an
artless, incorruptible innocence which was never really
in danger; Sheridan's sentimentalism in the handling of
this type of *mesálliance* is clear if we compare Lady
Teazle with her literal prototype, the exuberantly un-
faithful Mrs. Margery Pinchwife of brawny Wycherly's
Country Wife.

Or if we turn to the third and central ingredient of the
plot, the rival brothers, we find in Congreve, the Restoration writer, a ruthless and uncompromising realism. Congreve's villain Fainall (we note that it is the perfect
humour name for Joseph) is a slightly sinister figure,
whereas Joseph's evil consists mainly in intention and

word: the calculating Fainall actually succeeds in marrying for fortune (getting less than he bargained for) and practices his infidelities freely. The sentimental flavoring of Sheridan's disposition is further evident if we compare Congreve's Restoration hero Mirabell with the sentimental hero Charles. Both are the amatory centers of their respective plays, about whose persons and personalities female passions turn. Not only is Congreve's Mirabell a much more complex figure in his preoccupation with judgment, taste, character, and their place in conduct than is Charles, but he is a much less sentimental figure, being himself an aggressor upon the lives and happiness of such as Lady Wishfort and Mrs. Fainall and his own servant. He also may genuinely love Millamant, but he does not intend to sacrifice any part of her fortune to romance, and the marriage is not scheduled until every penny is guaranteed. Indeed, much of the "intrigue" of *The Way of the World* turns upon his stratagems for insuring that love will be invested at a solid profit. Moreover, we actually see Mirabell, the specimen of Restoration worldliness and elegance, betraying the man who is his habitual gaming companion with exemplary *sang froid*. He seduces the wife of this companion merely to while away the interval until he is sure of the fortune of the handsome lady who is to be his bride. And in the famous "proviso" scene between Mirabell and Millamant—the conditions to govern their marital life—we note mainly on the part of both a concern for their own privacy and independence.

In complete contrast to this type of worldly sanity and serenity and poise is Charles whose extravagances and follies seem more the overflowings of thoughtless "innocence" than of any excessive worldliness. We are *told* that he is a libertine, a drinker, a gambler, a pursuer of women; but of his wayward amours we glimpse only Lady Sneerwell, who appears to be the seducer, not the seduced. Whereas Mirabell is a cool practical head governing a tractable heart, Charles is a wooden head governed by a benevolent and gushing heart, a fountain of

golden compassion, at once kindly and whimsical. Mirabell craftily seeks money; Charles wantonly bestows it.
Yet Charles' thoughtless benevolence releases for him a
shower of gold, plenty beyond Mirabell's dreams. In
terms of Charles, Sheridan appears to say: love, gamble,
eat and drink—only be grateful and benevolent—and all
good things will be added unto you. The really profligate
rakes of Restoration Comedy modulate into the almost
ritualistically prodigal sons of Sentimental Comedy.
Charles (like Young Marlow of *She Stoops to Conquer*)
represents the accepted view that young men of spirit
and blood must sow an uncanonical oat or two before
being claimed for slippers, pipe, and fireside by comely
innocence. The prodigal son is a ritual figure because he
must make his mistakes before embracing the good life:
his sins are the inevitable ones of youthful inexperience,
not of a corrupt heart. Hence forgiveness and reconciliation are like rich garments flung over the sins and rags
of the prodigal son on his return.

The conception of Lady Teazle is not without its sentimentality. She does not, after all, capitulate to Joseph's
blandishments; in fact, we are given to believe that she
never really intended to do more than look, not to taste.
Wycherly's china souvenirs (symbols not only of accomplished, but relished adultery) are not distributed in
Sheridan's salon. Unlike Wycherly's country wife, Lady
Teazle is restored to the elderly arms of Sir Peter un-
blemished and repentant; true to the tradition of sentimental drama, she has her conversion to a more strict
life as a result of Sir Peter's quite gratuitous and all-too-
timely determination to supply her with money and independence. Her heart beats with the same gratitude for
Sir Peter's benevolence as does Charles's for his uncle's.
This is the sentimental heart overflowing with tender
gratitude; we are cheerfully expected to believe that these
transient cardiac tics will obliterate the abyss of years,
temperament, taste, habit and make a happy couple of
January and May.

One of the indices to sentimental comedy is the employment of the concepts of benevolence and gratitude. The eighteenth century regarded these emotions as the highest expressions of rational men, the transfiguring virtues which lifted him above the rest of the animal creation. Although Sheridan laughs at the "man of sentiment" in the person of Joseph, he exalts the tender, kindly, sentimental heart in the persons of Uncle Oliver, Maria, Charles, Sir Peter, and Lady Teazle.

The sentimentality of Sheridan's play can be better seen by comparing him to Fielding, whose *Tom Jones* appeared in 1748. With much the same combination of characters, Fielding faced much more realistically and unflinchingly the implications of the sentimental hero. For if the sentimental hero be a man acting mainly from impulse rather than from principle, then he is likely to be the victim of impulsive rashness or of impulses often a trifle unfragrant. Fielding presents to us such a man: drinking too much, wenching, brawling,—finally in indigence and despair, becoming a sort of kept gigolo for the enamored Lady Bellaston, something approaching a male prostitute. On the contrary, Sheridan's Charles, although much the same character, remains somehow a model of healthy, hearty bonhomie. Uncle Oliver pays off the mortgages and interest in rapturous admiration of such a good-hearted nephew. Fielding's logic of character would have required Charles to be on occasion crudely over-heavy in his cups, the successful seducer of Lady Teazle, the compensated companion of the enamoured and passionate Lady Sneerwell, and finally a sponging-house victim of unpaid debts.

Moreover it is strange that Joseph, the cool-hearted and prudent, the passionless man, should have so recklessly incurred the double risk of offending his sponsor Sir Peter and his lady-to-be Maria by an assignation with the frivolous Lady Teazle. It is what a thoughtless, irresponsible rake like Charles might have done. We note that in *Tom Jones* Young Blifil, the adroit and artful maneuverer, never takes such a risk. And we note also that it is Tom Jones who does become involved with many varieties of lady. Why then, we ask, does the gay, pleasure-loving, woman-magnetizing Charles not seek Lady Teazle whose dour husband already suspects him? And why does the sly, circumspect Joseph take risks that the prodigal Charles foregoes—especially as Charles remarks before the screen that he has no great scruples about such matters. The answer lies in Sheridan's great sentimentality: he cannot allow Charles the implications of his character. And what is notable is that Charles is in one sense Sheridan; and Sheridan did not hesitate to seek the comforts of beautiful ladies, even when the wives of his friends. Nor did he remain faithful even in sentiment to the remarkable women who were his wives. His comic vision is not that of his daily life and experience, but rather an expurgated one. Of course his own experience came much later, but it was the logical working out of his admiration for the Charles Surface type. Nor did his own Maria prevail over his wayward disposition.

The sentimental hero of his audience had to be at once worldly, experienced, full of impulse and heart, but yet a devil-of-a-fellow who never went far wrong, whose good heart had a built-in moral stabilizer. Hence although out of character, Joseph had in part to take over what were more naturally Charles's follies.

These observations do not constitute an adverse reflection on Sheridan's brilliant play. Like Wilde a century later, he is a comedian not of character but of situation and its manipulation. The incandescent brightness of his verbal dexterity easily blinds us to his superficial interest in character. The cleverness of the lines enchants us, and so infectious is Sheridan's gaiety and wit that even fops, such as Sir Benjamin Backbite, utter some of the best lines of the play.

In respect to the performance itself, it might be remembered that Sheridan's comedy had a topical element —that of scandal, one of the reasons presumably why he made that the titular element despite its being a minor element in the play. Sheridan's day was comparable to our own in that point: just as we have a number of "exposé" magazines which purport to give the inside low-down on the amours of celebrities, so in Sheridan's day contemporary journalism supplied readers with numerous instances of the scandalous chronicle. Indeed, Sheridan and his wife had been presumably the subjects of tittle-tattle and satiric dramatic representation: *The Maid of Bath* was a play directed in part at Elizabeth Linley, Sheridan's wife, and her relations with suitors prior to Brinsley. *The Town and Country Magazine* was particularly the contemporary journalistic buffet for serving scandal. It might be remembered that many of their allusions were factual as well as slanderous.

As for the performance, Sheridan was as fortunate in the first presentation of *The School for Scandal* as he had been unfortunate in his *Rivals*. All witnesses exclaim upon the perfection of the casting, a feature which was in part the skill of the more experienced Sheridan, if we are to believe James Boaden's words. The latter, quoted by R. Crompton Rhodes in *Harlequin Sheridan,* emphasizes that Sheridan was not only a more brilliant Congreve but while composing meditated on the individual personal graces and mannerisms of the players of the King's Company of the Theatre Royal of Drury Lane. Palmer, for example, who played the role of Joseph, was noted for a kind of plausible and polished insincerity of manner, sustained by a kind of "lingering sentiment." Smith, who played the role of Charles, was a product of Eton and the University, a mirror of fashionable manners and a man of "jovial sentiment" not unaided by liquor. King, as Sir Peter, was noted for his "caustic shyness," and Mrs. Abingdon, a Shavian Pygmalion and Fair Lady of her day who rose from a street-vending flower-girl to a fine lady of fashion and mirror of the beau monde, was admired for her "brilliant loquacity" as Lady Teazle. Maria had been intended for the noted Mary Robinson, who gracefully yielded her role to Priscilla Hopkins, noting in her Memoirs, "I was now so unshaped by my increasing size that I made my excuses."

Even minor characters were admirably portrayed. For example, "the gentleman's gentleman" was played by La Mash who was described by a contemporary as "the most elegantly made man I ever saw." Yates, bluff and salty, did the role of Sir Oliver, and Sir Benjamin Backbite was performed by Dodd, whose reputation for the role of the polished, genteel fop was at its height.

Finally, the reader must remember that one of the reasons for the importance of such an elegant and able cast was that of ritual: the performers of such a play appeared in brilliant court dress; their gestures, their stances, their postures were eloquent of elaborate, decorative, modish mannerism. They were like the figures in a brilliant tapestry, and as the critic Hazlitt reminds us, Sheridan's comedy was acted by clothes as well as people, by the "purple and fine raiment of the age of chivalry" before it was eclipsed by "the age of sophisters and calculators."

Sheridan's play, like Ibsen's *Doll House,* ended with a bang. It was said of Ibsen's play that when Nora slammed the door on the family at the end of the play it could be heard across Europe. When the screen fell in the last act of the *School for Scandal,* it could be literally heard across London, so immediate and concerted was the delighted response of the audience. Reynolds, a minor dramatist of the time, tells of his passing the Drury Lane theatre and hearing the sudden uproar. Thinking it a riot or the fall of a gallery or a fire, he investigated and found it nothing but the explosive pleasure and applause of the audience. The sound still reaches us across the decades, and we too respond with equal pleasure.

THE STAGING

Physically, the eighteenth century theatre was very much like that of our own day; it was, in fact the beginning of the modern theatre. The Renaissance and baroque drama of the preceding sixteenth and seventeenth centuries had possessed two quite different traditions. First, there were the popular plays presented commercially in theatres often improvised from inn-yards and indoor tennis courts. Here, as far as production was concerned, the rule of economy prevailed and there was a minimum of scenery. The audience, standing in the "pit" or seated in the encircling galleries, surrounded the actors, who performed mainly on an apron platform that projected well out from the stage proper. But if the physical characteristics of the popular theatre were meager, the intellectual and psychological ones were not. The intricacy of Renaissance plots is famous, as is the richness and variety of metaphor in the actors' lines.

The second tradition which developed during the years preceding the eighteenth century was that of the court gala, especially gotten up to celebrate the marriage or coronation of some member of the ruling family. Here, elaborate scenery and costumes were primary attractions, and no expense was spared. Fantastic palaces, at the wink of an eye, were changed into gushing fountains, rocky eyries, or distant battlefields. The actors in these masques (as they were called) were sometimes professional, but often members of the court; even kings and queens took part. Needless to say, no great histrionic demands were made upon the participants. Indeed, in a masque, the plot was perhaps the least significant consideration.

In the eighteenth century these two traditions united into one which still persists today. From the popular theatres of Shakespeare and Molière came the notion of a highly plotted narrative demanding considerable acting ability; and from the court masque came the tradition of quickly changing painted scenery.

In England, with the eventual relaxation of the 1737 law which governed the licensing of public performances, the popular theatre could operate more freely. Theatregoing became a fashionable recreation, and producers in the so-called "illegitimate" houses were able to realize a profit even in their smaller auditoriums. In London there were buildings such as the Opera House in Haymarket boasting enormous stages which could accommodate the full machinery for descending clouds and rushing rivers — effects still called for in Italian operas. But most eighteenth century theatres were more modest in their dimensions; often their stages were tiny by modern standards. Sometimes there was barely room for the actors.

Whether the stage was large or small, the scenic equipment was something like this. On either side of the stage was a set of wooden frames, which could run on and off stage in grooves in the floor, suspended overhead on a wheel and track system such as we sometimes see used for sliding barn doors. These wooden frames were covered with canvas and hid the offstage portions of the theatre. They were called "wings." Much larger frames, called "flats," operated in the same way but met in the center to provide the back wall of the set. Across the top of each set of wings was a canvas strip called a "border" which extended across the stage and served as masking to hide the upper part of the stage house from the audience. All these scenic elements were painted to represent some indoor or outdoor scene.

When the locale of the play had to be changed, the wings and flats could be drawn offstage in their grooves, revealing another set of flats and wings with a different scene painted on them. All details of a given scene were painted on the flats, even furniture and properties, except for those objects which the actors actually used. Eighteenth century actors rarely sat down so there was not apt to be much furniture about.

The stage opening, or proscenium arch, was often elaborately decorated, and usually boxes for the spectators were housed in it. From these box seats you could easily look down on the apron, but you could not see the stage proper without craning your neck. This indicates that the apron was where the actors spent most of their time, the area behind being reserved mainly for scenery. Thus the eighteenth century stage-setting was more of a *backing*

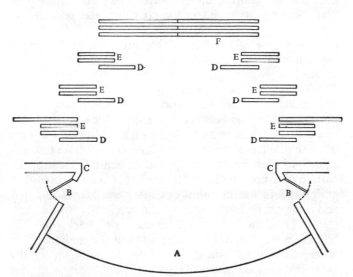

Diagram of a typical late eighteenth-century stage

A is the apron upon which most of the action took place; B, the proscenium doors; C, the proscenium opening behind which the curtain hung. The onstage wings are marked D, and those off-stage, awaiting their turn to be used, are marked E. Behind the first set of wings are a pair of shutters which can close the stage completely off for scenes in hallways and other constricted quarters. The back shutters are marked F.

for the actor, in contrast to the modern set, which *encloses* him. On each side of the proscenium arch was a door which led from the offstage area to the apron. Actors made their entrances and exits through these doors or through the spaces between the wings.

The audience not only occupied the normal orchestra seats, but also several tiers of boxes which curved around the inside of the auditorium like giant horse-shoes with their open ends toward the stage. Many of the older theatres in this country, such as the Metropolitan Opera House in New York (1882) still retain this horse-shoe arrangement for box seats and balconies. This form may have had its origin in the converted inn-yards where popular theatre was staged in the sixteenth and seventeenth centuries.

This picture of a typical eighteenth century theatre, as we remarked at the beginning, reminds us of a modern theatre, especially compared to what had gone before. But if our theatres have changed only a little and if we still occasionally use wing and border sets, there are important differences between our method of staging a play and the traditional method of the eighteenth century. One of these differences involves a whole new attitude towards change of scenery. In the eighteenth century theatre, the curtain was not closed at the end of a scene. Instead, a uniformed factotum came out after the actors had left and removed or rearranged all the properties for the next scene. Then the wings and shutters slid back, and the borders were raised *a vista* (in sight of the audience) by unseen hands backstage, revealing the new set in the manner described above. These *a vista* changes were part of the fun of going to the theatre, and audiences might well have felt cheated if the curtain had hidden them. As a matter of fact, this popular relic of baroque theatre practice did not disappear until the last century.

While the modern theatre-goer, schooled in the complete representationalism of Hollywood and Broadway, may object that these painted scenes must rarely have been very convincing, let him remember that the revealing brilliance of modern electric lighting did not yet exist. Eighteenth century scenery was lighted only by the flickering of myriads of candles. Chandeliers were hung backstage between the wings and borders, and also out in the auditorium. These auditorium lights, by the way, were *not* extinguished during performances.

Another important difference between eighteenth century practice and our own lies in the sphere of costume. In the eighteenth century no distinction was made between "modern dress" and "period" productions. An actor, whether he played Hamlet or an eighteenth century gentleman, wore either everyday dress or a kind of special "actor's costume" such as we see in Watteau's paintings of Italian comedians. One actress of the period, it is recorded, did give a Roman matron the classic toga she deserved, but insisted on wearing it over a hoopskirt!

This everyday eighteenth century dress was quite elaborate, however. Men wore black or white silk stockings and pumps decorated with fancy buckles. Their trousers consisted of tight breeches buckled just below the knee. They also wore capacious waistcoats and jackets with skirts or tails in back which descended to the knees. Lace bands were worn at the neck and lace cuffs at the wrists. The three-cornered hat with cockade or feather and the inevitable white-powdered tie-wig topped off the ensemble. The men of the eighteenth century had no compunctions about wearing bright and highly decorated materials, brocaded or printed in strong and colorful patterns. The tradition of black, brown, and gray which now dominates men's everyday dress did not set in until the nineteenth century.

Women wore pumps, too, and long stiff skirts and bodices as colorful as the men's suits. Skirts were almost always worn over hoops, and were often split up the center to reveal a contrasting underskirt. Sometimes panniers (wicker or wire frames which expanded the apparent width of the hips) were worn instead of hoopskirts. Over these the skirts were often draped in festoons which could end in short trains. Women's bodices were cut to a sharp point at the waist and in a very low curved or square neckline. Sleeves were elbow length, terminating in lace ruffles. White powdered wigs, very high, were worn by all fashionable women for dress occasions, often in combination with plumes.

The elegant everyday dress, the *a vista* scene change (which probably groaned and creaked enormously), the lighted auditorium, and above all the artificial quality of the painted wings and flats — these things are to be kept in mind when we try to reconstruct the production of eighteenth century plays. Remember, too, that the play was not a classic when it first appeared. Audiences did not listen in worshipful silence. Perhaps they found themselves more amusing than the play: at any rate they were apt to chatter during many of the scenes, and only during the most important speeches by favorite actors and actresses was there absolute silence. During these scenes the fans punctuated every particularly good line with salvos of applause. At the end of the play the manager would come out on the apron and if he was greeted with hisses and boos he would retire in defeat, knowing that the play was a failure and that it could not be repeated. If, on the other hand, the audience's reception was reasonably enthusiastic, he would announce triumphantly: "The unparalleled success of the latest and brightest spark from the anvil of the comic muse will be repeated every evening until further notice."

For the eighteenth century audience, the theatre was more than a playhouse; it was a place where invitations were issued, assignations made, duels arranged, debutantes introduced, dowries settled, and reputations made and lost. It was a glittering spectacle of fashionable dress and histrionic partisanship.

A PORTRAIT

*Addressed to Mrs. Crewe[1], with the Comedy
of the School for Scandal*

BY R. B. SHERIDAN, ESQ.

Tell me, ye prim adepts in Scandal's school,
Who rail by precept, and detract by rule,
Lives there no character, so tried, so known,
So deck'd with grace, and so unlike your own,
That even you assist her fame to raise,
Approve by envy, and by silence praise?
Attend! — a model shall attract your view—
Daughters of calumny, I summon you!
You shall decide if this a portrait prove,
Or fond creation of the Muse and Love.
Attend, ye virgin critics, shrewd and sage,
Ye matron censors of this childish age,
Whose peering eye and wrinkled front declare
A fixed antipathy to young and fair;
By cunning, cautious; or by nature, cold,
In maiden madness, virulently bold!
Attend! ye skilled to coin the precious tale,
Creating proof, where innuendos fail!
Whose practised memories, cruelly exact,
Omit no circumstance, except the fact!
Attend all ye who boast — or old or young
The living libel of a slanderous tongue!
So shall my theme as far contrasted be,
As saints by fiends, or hymns by calumny.
Come, gentle Amoret[2] (for 'neath that name,

---

[1] An extraordinarily beautiful woman, Frances Anne, daughter
of Fulke Greville, married to John Crewe in 1776. She was a
celebrated beauty of the day, much seen with Sheridan and the
occasion of scandalous speculation concerning the intimacy of
their relationship.

[2] Mrs. Crewe.

In worthier verse is sung thy beauty's fame);
Come—for but thee who seeks the Muse? and while
Celestial blushes check thy conscious smile,
With timid grace and hesitating eye,
The perfect model, which I boast, supply.
Vain Muse! couldst thou the humblest sketch create
Of her, or slightest charm couldst imitate—
Could thy blest strain in kindred colors trace
The faintest wonder of her form and face—
Poets would study the immortal line,
And *Reynolds*[3] own *his* art subdued by thine;
That art, which well might added lustre give
To Nature's best, and Heaven's superlative:
On Granby's cheek might bid new glories rise,
Or point a purer beam from Devon's[4] eyes!
Hard is the task to shape that beauty's praise,
Whose judgment scorns the homage flattery pays!
But praising Amoret we cannot err,
No tongue o'ervalues Heaven, or flatters her!
Yet she by Fate's perverseness—she alone
Would doubt our truth, nor deem such praise her own!
Adorning Fashion, unadorn'd by dress,
Simple from taste, and not from carelessness;
Discreet in gesture, in deportment mild,
Not stiff with prudence, nor uncouthly wild:
No state has *Amoret!* no studied mien;
She frowns no *goddess,* and she moves no *queen.*
The softer charm that in her manner lies
Is framed to captivate, yet not surprise;
It justly suits th'expression of her face—
'Tis less than dignity, and more than grace!
On her pure cheek the native hue is such,
That form'd by Heav'n to be admired so much,
The hand divine, with a less partial care,

---

[3] Sir Joshua Reynolds, famous portrait painter of the eighteenth century, did three portraits of her.

[4] The Marchioness of Granby, painted four times by Reynolds, and the handsome Duchess of Devonshire are included in the flattery.

Might well have fix'd a fainter crimson there.
And bade the gentle inmate of her breast—
Inshrined Modesty!—supply the rest.
But who the peril of her lips shall paint?
Strip them of smiles—still, still all words are faint!
But moving Love himself appears to teach
Their action, though denied to rule her speech;
And thou who seest her speak and dost not hear,
Mourn not her distant accents 'scape thine ear;
Viewing those lips, thou still may'st make pretence
To judge of what she says, and swear 'tis sense:
Cloth'd with such grace, and such expression fraught,
They move in meaning, and they pause in thought!
But dost thou farther watch, with charm'd surprise,
The mild irresolution of her eyes,
Curious to mark how frequent they repose,
In brief eclipse and momentary close—
Ah, seest thou not an ambush'd Cupid there,
Too tim'rous of his charge, with jealous care
Veils and unveils those beams of heav'nly light,
Too full, too fatal else, for mortal sight?
Nor yet, such pleasing vengeance fond to meet,
In pard'ning dimples hope a safe retreat.
What though her peaceful breasts should ne'er allow
Subduing frowns to arm her alter'd brow,
By Love, I swear, and by his gentle wiles,
More fatal still the mercy of her smiles!
Thus lovely, thus adorn'd, possessing all
Of bright or fair that can to woman fall.
The height of vanity might well be thought
Prerogative in her, and Nature's fault.
Yet gentle *Amoret,* in mind supreme
As well as charms, rejects the vainer theme;
And half mistrustful of her beauty's store,
She barbs with wit those darts too keen before:—
Read in all knowledge that her sex should reach,
Though *Greville,*[5] or the *Muse,* should deign to teach,

---

[5] Mrs. Crewe's mother, to whom Sheridan dedicated his play *The Critic.*

Fond to improve, nor tim'rous to discern
How far it is a woman's grace to learn;
In *Millar's*[6] dialect she would not prove
Apollo's priestess, but Apollo's love,
Graced by those signs, which truth delights to own,
The timid blush, and mild submitted tone:
Whate'er she says, though sense appear throughout,
Displays the tender hue of female doubt;
Deck'd with that charm, how lovely wit appears,
How graceful *science,* when that robe she wears!
Such too her talents, and her bent of mind,
As speak a sprightly heart by thought refined,
A taste for mirth, by contemplation school'd,
A turn for ridicule, by candour ruled,
A scorn of folly, which she tries to hide;
An awe of talent, which she owns with pride!
Peace! idle Muse, no more thy strains prolong,
But yield a theme, thy warmest praises wrong;
Just to her merit, though thou canst not raise
Thy feeble voice, behold th'acknowledged praise
Has spread conviction through the envious train,
And cast a fatal gloom o'er Scandal's reign!
And lo! each pallid hag, with blister'd tongue,
Mutters assent to all thy zeal has sung—
Owns all the colors just—the outline true;
Thee my inspirer, and my *model*—CREWE!

---

[6] Lady Millar wrote verses, held literary salons, and had at her home an elegant vase into which her guests, including Sheridan, dropped poetic contributions.

CAST OF CHARACTERS

in the order of their appearance

LADY SNEERWELL, a wealthy widow and Society leader.

SNAKE, a professional hanger-on.

JOSEPH SURFACE, a young aristocrat of propriety and sentiment, Sir Oliver Surface's orphaned nephew, sometimes addressed as MR. SURFACE as senior living member of his family.

MARIA, pretty and ingenuous young ward of Sir Peter Teazle.

MRS. CANDOUR, a fashionable member of Lady Sneerwell's circle.

CRABTREE, a gentleman of leisure, another intimate of the clique.

SIR BENJAMIN BACKBITE, his dashing young nephew.

SIR PETER TEAZLE, an aging, unpretentious, wealthy gentleman; Maria's guardian.

JOSEPH SURFACE

ROWLEY, a sober and sensible businessman, formerly steward to the deceased father of Joseph and Charles Surface.

LADY TEAZLE, Sir Peter's frivolous young wife.

SIR PETER TEAZLE

MARIA

SIR OLIVER SURFACE, Sir Peter's lifelong friend, uncle of the orphaned Joseph and Charles Surface.

TRIP, elegant footman to Charles Surface.

LADY TEAZLE

CHARLES SURFACE

MOSES, a money lender.

CHARLES SURFACE, wastrel younger brother of Joseph, Sir Oliver's nephew.

CARELESS, a gay young blade, bosom companion to Charles.

SIR HARRY BUMPER, a casual drinking and gaming companion of Charles.

TWO GENTLEMEN, unnamed cronies of Charles.

also FOOTMEN, described as "SERVANTS" in Sheridan's script, and Lady Teazle's personal MAID.

MOSES

SYNOPSIS OF SCENES

The action takes place in fashionable London (in the vicinity of Grosvenor Square) in the 1770's. Although the actual timing of the individual scenes is not given, Sheridan intended the entire action to take place within "a single revolution of the sun" in conformity with Aristotle's dictum in the *Poetics*. The timing of the scenes suggested below follows hints given in the text with allowances for reasonable intervals between when indicated.

ACT I.

Scene 1. Lady Sneerwell's Dressing Room (mid-morning).

Scene 2. Sir Peter Teazle's Library (shortly afterward).

ACT II.

Scene 1. A Room in Sir Peter Teazle's House (early in the same afternoon).

Scene 2. Lady Sneerwell's Parlor (about 2 P.M.).

Scene 3. The Reception Room in Sir Peter Teazle's House (later).

ACT III.

Scene 1. Sir Peter Teazle's Library (immediately following the preceding scene).

Scene 2. The Reception Room in Charles Surface's House (about 4 P.M.).

Scene 3. The Game Room (immediately following).

ACT IV.

Scene 1. The Picture Room in Charles Surface's House (immediately following).

Scene 2. The Parlor in Charles Surface's House (immediately following).

Scene 3. The Library in Joseph Surface's House (tea-time).

ACT V.

PROLOGUE

written by Mr. Garrick[1]

A SCHOOL FOR SCANDAL! tell me, I beseech you,
Needs there a school this modish art to teach you?
No need of lessons now, the knowing think;
We might as well be taught to eat and drink.
Caused by a dearth of scandal, should the vapors[2]
Distress our fair ones—let them read the papers;
Their powerful mixtures such disorders hit;
Crave what you will—there's *quantum sufficit*.[3]
"Lord!" cries my Lady *Wormwood* (who loves tattle,
And puts much salt and pepper in her prattle),
Just ris'n at noon, all night at cards when threshing
Strong tea and scandal—"Bless me, how refreshing!
"Give me the papers, *Lisp*—how bold and free! (sips)
"Last night Lord L. (sips) was caught with Lady D.
"For aching heads what charming sal volatile![4] *(sips)*
"If Mrs. B. will still continue flirting,
"We hope she'll DRAW, or we'll UNDRAW the
    curtain.
'Fine satire, poz[5]—in public all abuse it,
"Now *Lisp*, read you—there at that dash and star."[6]
"Yes, ma'm—*A certain lord had best beware,*
"Who lives not twenty miles from Grosvenor Square;
"For should he Lady W. find willing,
'*Wormwood is bitter"*—"Oh, that's me, the villain!
"Throw it behind the fire, and never more

---

1 David Garrick, celebrated actor, manager, and playwright.

2 A fashionable female ailment: melancholy or "the blues."

3 "As much as is necessary," a pharmaceutical direction.

4 Smelling salts.

5 Positively.

6 The Scandal Sheet method of suggesting names, such as
Lady S—*.

"Let that vile paper come within the door."
Thus at our friends we laugh, who feel the dart;
To reach our feelings, we ourselves must smart.
Is our young bard so young, to think that he
Can stop the full spring-tide of calumny?
Knows he the world so little, and its trade?
Alas! the devil's sooner raised than laid.
So strong, so swift, the monster there's no gagging:
Cut Scandal's head off, still the tongue is wagging.
Proud of your smiles once lavishly bestow'd,
Again our young Don Quixote[7] takes the road;
To show his gratitude he draws his pen,
And seeks this hydra,[8] Scandal, in his den.
For your applause all perils he will through—
He'll fight—that's write—a cavalliero true,
Till every drop of blood—that's ink—is spilt for you.

---

[7] Sheridan, the "young bard" whose play *The Rivals* had won such acclaim, is compared to the mad dreamer of Spanish fiction.

[8] Multiple-headed monster of Greek mythology.

ACT ONE

Scene One

Lady Sneerwell's Dressing Room where, in accordance with the mode established by the SALONS *of the* GRANDES DAMES *of French Society, she frequently entertains her intimates to relieve the tedium of being idly rich. The richly paneled rear wall is broken by an ornamental curtained arch which leads to her bedroom. The entrance at the left leads to a hall and stairway to the ground floor. Off the wings to the right are other rooms in this elaborate London mansion. Lady Sneerwell sits at her dressing table on the right. The practical details of making herself enchanting have been accomplished, but she knows that the pretense of being in the process of completing her toilet lends piquancy to the intimacy of the scandalous conversation in which she revels. Her fawning toady Mr. Snake daintily sips a cup of chocolate as he reports on the progress of the campaign of reputation-destruction which is being waged. Lady Sneerwell is a handsome woman in her forties, affecting the period's fashionable elaborate headdress, pinched waist, and voluminous skirts. Snake is discreetly sombre except for his white ruffled shirt: he wears a black coat, waistcoat and trousers, black silk stockings and pumps. From his costume, audiences can detect that he is not on the side of the angels. The opening of the curtain discovers them in the midst of their plottings.*

LADY SNEERWELL: *(intent on the business of the moment)* The paragraphs, you say, Mr. Snake, were all inserted?

SNAKE: *(in a tone of modest self-confidence)* They

were, madam; and as I copied them myself in a feigned hand, there can be no suspicion whence they came.

LADY SNEERWELL: Did you circulate the report of Lady Brittle's intrigue with Captain Boastall?

SNAKE: *(with pardonable self-satisfaction)* That's in as fine a train as your ladyship could wish. In the common course of things, I think it must reach Mrs. Clackitt's ears within four-and-twenty hours; *(knowingly)* and then, you know, the business is as good as done.

LADY SNEERWELL: *(thoughtfully)* Why, truly, Mrs. Clackitt has a very pretty talent, and a great deal of industry.

SNAKE: *(with urbane detachment)* True, madam, and has been tolerably successful in her day. To my knowledge she has been the cause of six matches broken off, and three sons disinherited; *(putting down his cup to concentrate on his statistics)* of four forced elopements, and as many close confinements;[1] nine separate maintenances,[2] and two divorces. Nay, I have more than once traced her causing a *tete-a-tete* in the *Town and Country Magazine*,[3] when the parties, perhaps, had never seen each other's faces before in the course of their lives.

LADY SNEERWELL: *(resenting the implication of Mrs. Clackitt's superiority)* She certainly has talents, but her manner is gross.

SNAKE: *(soothingly)* 'Tis very true. *(assuming the attitude of an art critic)* She generally designs well, has a free tongue, and a bold invention; but her coloring is too dark, and her outlines are often extravagant. *(with sincere flattery)* She wants that delicacy of tint, and mellowness of sneer, which distinguishes your ladyship's scandal.

LADY SNEERWELL: *(appeased)* You are partial, Snake.

SNAKE: *(pressing his advantage)* Not in the least; every-

---

[1] Confinements because of imminent childbirth.

[2] Separate dwellings for husband and wife.

[3] Begun in 1769, the *Tete-a-tete* was an ingenious monthly feature of the magazine in which a sketch of two socially prominent individuals was followed by an imaginary conversation between them suggesting a scandalous and fashionable intrigue.

To my knowledge she has been the cause of six matches broken off, and three sons disinherited; of four forced elopements . . .

body allows that Lady Sneerwell can do more with a word or a look than many can with the most labored detail, even when they happen to have a little truth on their side to support it.

LADY SNEERWELL: *(with unusual candor)* Yes, my dear Snake; and I am no hypocrite to deny the satisfaction I reap from the success of my efforts. Wounded myself in the early part of my life by the envenomed tongue of slander, I confess I have since known no pleasure equal to the reducing others to the level of my own injured reputation.

SNAKE: *(agreeably)* Nothing can be more natural. *(with pretended casualness)* But, Lady Sneerwell, there is one affair in which you have lately employed me, wherein, I confess, I am at a loss to guess your motives.

LADY SNEERWELL: I conceive you mean with respect to my neighbor, Sir Peter Teazle, and his family?

SNAKE: *(forthrightly)* I do. Here are two young men, to whom Sir Peter has acted as a kind of guardian since their father's death; the elder possessing the most amiable character, and universally well-spoken of; the younger, the most dissipated and extravagant young fellow in the kingdom, without friends or character: the former an avowed admirer of your ladyship, and apparently your favorite; the latter attached to Maria, Sir Peter's ward, and confessedly beloved by her. *(deeply puzzled)* Now, on the face of these circumstances, it is utterly unaccountable to me, why you, the widow of a city knight, with a good jointure,[4] should not close with the passion of a man of such character and expectations as Mr. Surface; and more so why you should be so uncommonly earnest to destroy the mutual attachment subsisting between his brother Charles and Maria.

LADY SNEERWELL: *(blandly)* Then at once to unravel this mystery, I must inform you that love has no share whatever in the intercourse between Mr. Surface and me.

SNAKE: *(seemingly surprised)* No!

---

[4] Her wealthy husband, knighted because of some patriotic service, had provided well for his widow.

LADY SNEERWELL: *(continuing her revelation)* His real attachment is to Maria, *(cynically)* or her fortune; but finding in his brother a favored rival, he has been obliged to mask his pretensions, and profit by my assistance.

SNAKE: Yet still I am more puzzled why you should interest yourself in his success.

LADY SNEERWELL: *(delighted to confess her secrets to a trusted intimate)* How dull you are! Cannot you surmise the weakness which I hitherto, through shame, have concealed even from you? Must I confess that Charles, that libertine, that extravagant, that bankrupt in fortune and reputation, that he it is for whom I'm thus anxious and malicious, and to gain whom I would sacrifice everything?

SNAKE: *(pleased at obtaining her confession—)* Now, indeed, your conduct appears consistent; *(—but probing for more)* but how came you and Mr. Surface so confidential?

LADY SNEERWELL: For our mutual interest. I have found him out a long time since. *(rather pleased by her own keenness)* I know him to be artful, selfish, and malicious; in short, a sentimental knave; while with Sir Peter, and indeed with all his acquaintance, he passes for a youthful miracle of prudence, good sense, and benevolence.

SNAKE: *(sharing her understanding of the real Joseph Surface)* Yes; yet Sir Peter vows he has not his equal in England; and above all, he praises him as a man of sentiment.

LADY SNEERWELL: *(nodding)* True; and with the assistance of his sentiment and hypocrisy, he has brought Sir Peter entirely into his interest with regard to Maria; while poor Charles has no friend in the house, though, I fear, he has a powerful one in Maria's heart, against whom we must direct our schemes.

Their plotting is interrupted by the entrance of a servant from the left, dressed in traditional footman's livery.

SERVANT: *(announcing)* Mr. Surface.

LADY SNEERWELL: Show him up.

The servant bows slightly and leaves to escort Joseph to the boudoir while Lady Sneerwell resumes her primping. The footman reappears with the guest, signals him to enter with a dignified gesture, and departs. Joseph Surface gives every appearance of an intelligent and serious young man, upholding the highest principles and deeply concerned with the well-being of others. His black coat, white waistcoat, black silk stockings and pumps indicate his outward sobriety and also classify him with Snake in the eyes of the audience. That he is a man of fashion is evidenced by the elegant cut and precise tailoring of his dress. Nothing about him, save possibly his over-meticulous observance of form, hints at his hypocrisy. He advances to bestow a formal kiss on the hand of his hostess.

JOSEPH: *(solicitously)* My dear Lady Sneerwell, how do you do today? *(turns to bow to the other guest)* Mr. Snake, your most obedient.[5] *(Snake bows very low.)*

LADY SNEERWELL: Snake has just been rallying me on our mutual attachment; but I have informed him of our real views. You know how useful he has been to us, and, believe me, the confidence is not ill placed. *(Snake acknowledges her reference to him with a bow.)*

JOSEPH: *(quickly suppressing the suggestion of a frown and bowing to Snake)* Madam, it is impossible for me to suspect a man of Mr. Snake's sensibility and discernment. *(Snake returns the bow.)*

LADY SNEERWELL: *(vivaciously)* Well, well, no compliments now; but tell me when you saw your mistress, Maria; or what is more material to me, your brother.

JOSEPH: I have not seen either since I left you; but I can inform you that they never meet. Some of your stories have taken a good effect on Maria.

LADY SNEERWELL: *(turning to Snake)* Ah! my dear

---

[5] The usual abbreviated form of the polite salutation "your most obedient servant."

Snake! the merit of this belongs to you; *(Snake bows again to Joseph.)* but do your brother's distresses increase?

JOSEPH: Every hour. I am told he has had another execution[6] in the house yesterday. In short, his dissipation and extravagance exceed anything I have ever heard of.

LADY SNEERWELL: *(tenderly)* Poor Charles!

JOSEPH: *(so habitually hypocritical that he forgets whom he is addressing)* True, madam; notwithstanding his vices, one can't help feeling for him. Poor Charles! *(sighs)* I'm sure I wish it were in my power to be of any essential service to him; for the man who does not share in the distresses of a brother, *(carried away by the nobility of his pronouncement)* even though merited by his own misconduct, deserves—

LADY SNEERWELL: *(interrupting with some exasperation)* Oh, Lud! you are going to be moral, and forget that you are among friends.

JOSEPH: Egad, that's true! I'll keep that sentiment till I see Sir Peter; however, it certainly is a charity to rescue Maria from such a libertine, who, if he is to be reclaimed, can be so only by a person of your ladyship's superior accomplishments and understanding. *(During this speech sounds are heard below indicating the arrival of another caller.)*

SNAKE: I believe, Lady Sneerwell, here's company coming; I'll go copy the letter I mentioned to you. *(bows to kiss Lady Sneerwell's hand, then bows to Joseph)* Mr. Surface, your most obedient. *(He bows his way out to the right.)*

JOSEPH: *(returning the bow)* Sir, your very devoted. *(Pauses a moment to make certain that Snake is out of earshot and betrays irritability as he turns abruptly to Lady Sneerwell)* Lady Sneerwell, I am very sorry you have put any further confidence in that fellow.

---

[6] Seizure of furnishings and personal property for non-payment of bills.

LADY SNEERWELL: *(annoyed at the reprimand)* Why so?

JOSEPH: I have lately detected him in frequent conference with old Rowley, who was formerly my father's steward, and has never, you know, been a friend of mine.

LADY SNEERWELL: *(obviously disturbed)* And do you think he would betray us?

JOSEPH: Nothing more likely; take my word for't, Lady Sneerwell, that fellow hasn't virtue enough to be faithful even to his own villainy. *(The hasty interlude is interrupted by his awareness of the approach of Maria whom he recognizes just before her entrance at the left.)* Ah! Maria!

Maria's entrance is somewhat breathless. She is young, fresh, and pretty. In spite of being Sir Peter's ward, she has never learned to dissemble; her native honesty and ingenuousness seem out of place in this worldly atmosphere.

LADY SNEERWELL: Maria, my dear, how do you do? What's the matter?

MARIA: Oh! there is that disagreeable lover of mine, Sir Benjamin Backbite, has just called at my guardian's, with his odious uncle Crabtree; so I slipped out, and ran hither to avoid them.

LADY SNEERWELL: Is that all?

JOSEPH: *(betraying his jealousy)* If my brother Charles had been of the party, madam, perhaps you would not have been so much alarmed.

LADY SNEERWELL: Nay, now you are severe; for I dare swear the truth of the matter is, Maria heard *you* were here. But, my dear, what has Sir Benjamin done, that you would avoid him so?

MARIA: Oh, he has done nothing; but 'tis for what he has said: his conversation is perpetual libel on all his acquaintance.

JOSEPH: *(determined to be agreeable to the woman he hopes to marry)* Ay, and the worst of it is, there is no advantage in not knowing him; for he'll abuse a stranger just as soon as his best friend; and his uncle's as bad.

LADY SNEERWELL: Nay, but we should make allowance; Sir Benjamin is a wit and a poet.

MARIA: For my part, I confess, madam, wit loses its respect with me, when I see it in company with malice. What do you think, Mr. Surface?

JOSEPH: Certainly, madam; to smile at the jest which plants a thorn in another's breast is to become a principal in the mischief.

LADY SNEERWELL: Pshaw! there's no possibility of being witty without a little ill nature: the malice of a good thing is the barb that makes it stick. What's your opinion, Mr. Surface?

JOSEPH: *(experiencing no difficulty in providing a "sentiment")* To be sure, madam; that conversation where the spirit of raillery is suppressed, will ever appear tedious and insipid.

MARIA: *(somewhat in awe of her obvious superiors but determined to voice her real feelings)* Well, I'll not debate how far scandal may be allowable; but in a man, I am sure, it is always contemptible. We have pride, envy, rivalship, and a thousand motives to depreciate each other; but the male slanderer must have the cowardice of a woman before he can traduce one.

The servant appears at the door to make an announcement.

SERVANT: Madam, Mrs. Candour is below, and if your ladyship's at leisure, will leave her carriage.

LADY SNEERWELL: Beg her to walk in. *(The servant bows and leaves.)* Now, Maria, here is a character to your taste; for though Mrs. Candour is a little talkative, everybody allows her to be the best-natured and best sort of woman.

MARIA: *(nettled by the whole tenor of the conversation)* Yes, with a very gross affectation of good nature and benevolence, she does more mischief than the direct malice of Old Crabtree.

JOSEPH: *(intent on recovering Maria's approbation)* I' faith that's true, Lady Sneerwell: whenever I hear the current running against the characters of my friends, I never think them in such danger as when Candour undertakes their defense.

LADY SNEERWELL: Hush! here she is!

Mrs. Candour sweeps into the room, large, tempestuous, gushing. She gives the immediate impression of the older society woman whose only pleasure in life is gossip prompted by secret envy.

MRS. CANDOUR: *(assuming the center of the stage instantly)* My dear Lady Sneerwell, how have you been this century? Mr. Surface, what news do you hear? though indeed it is no matter, for I think one hears nothing else but scandal.

JOSEPH: Just so, indeed, ma'am.

MRS. CANDOUR: Oh, Maria! child, what, is the whole affair off between you and Charles? His extravagance, I presume; the town talks of nothing else.

MARIA: *(inwardly incensed, coldly)* Indeed! I am very sorry, ma'am, the town is not better employed.

MRS. CANDOUR: *(stimulated by disapprobation, with good nature)* True, true, child; but there's no stopping people's tongues. I own I was hurt to hear it, as I indeed was to learn, from the same quarter, that your guardian, Sir Peter, and Lady Teazle have not agreed lately as well as could be wished.

MARIA: 'Tis strangely impertinent for people to busy themselves so.

MRS. CANDOUR: Very true, child; but what's to be done? People will talk; there's no preventing it. Why, it was but yesterday I was told Miss Gadabout had eloped with Sir Filigree Flirt. But, Lord! there's no minding what one hears; though, to be sure, I had this from very good authority.

MARIA: *(thoroughly disgusted)* Such reports are highly scandalous.

MRS. CANDOUR: *(impervious)* So they are, child; shameful! shameful! But the world is so censorious, no character escapes. Lord, now who would have suspected your friend, Miss Prim, of an indiscretion? Yet such is the ill-nature of people, that they say her uncle stopped her last week, just as she was stepping into the York diligence[7] with her dancing-master.

MARIA: *(indignantly)* I'll answer for't there are no grounds for that report.

MRS. CANDOUR: *(agreeably)* Ah, no foundation in the world, I dare swear: no more, probably than for the story circulated last month, of Mrs. Festino's affair with Colonel Cassino; though, to be sure, that matter was never rightly cleared up.

JOSEPH: *(partly playing up to Maria but also preserving his reputation as a man of exalted sentiment)* The license of invention some people take is monstrous indeed.

MARIA: 'Tis so; but, in my opinion, those who report such things are equally culpable.

MRS. CANDOUR: *(magnificently fatalistic)* To be sure they are; tale-bearers are as bad as the tale-makers; 'tis an old observation, and a very true one. But what's to be done, as I said before? How will you prevent people from talking? Today, Mrs. Clackitt assured me, Mr. and Mrs. Honeymoon were at last become mere man and wife, like the rest of their acquaintance. She likewise hinted that a certain widow, in the next street, had to get rid of her dropsy and recovered her shape in a most surprising manner. And at the same time, Miss Tattle, who was by, affirmed that Lord Buffalo had discovered his lady at a house of no extraordinary fame; and that Sir Harry Bouquet and Tom Saunter were to measure swords on a similar provocation. But, Lord, do you think I would report these things? No, no! tale-bearers, as I said before, are just as bad as the tale-makers.

JOSEPH: *(with no outward semblance of being ironical)* Ah, Mrs. Candour, if everybody had your forbearance and good nature!

MRS. CANDOUR: I confess, Mr. Surface, I cannot bear to hear people attacked behind their backs; and when ugly circumstances come out against our acquaintance, I own I always love to think the best. *(suddenly reminded*

---

[7] The London to York Mail, fastest conveyance, "sports car" of 1775.

that she is almost overlooking a scandalous tidbit directly at hand) By-the-bye, I hope 'tis not true that your brother is absolutely ruined?

JOSEPH: *(with pious resignation and affected reluctance to discuss the matter)* I am afraid his circumstances are very bad indeed, ma'am.

MRS. CANDOUR: Ah! I heard so; but you must tell him to keep up his spirits; everybody almost is the same way —Lord Spindle, Sir Thomas Splint, Captain Quinze, and Mr. Nickit—all up, I hear, within this week; so if Charles is undone, he'll find half his acquaintance ruined too, and that, you know, is a consolation.

JOSEPH: Doubtless, ma'am; a very great one.

The servant enters from the left to announce two more guests and departs.

SERVANT: Mr. Crabtree and Sir Benjamin Backbite.

LADY SNEERWELL: *(teasingly)* So, Maria, you see your lover pursues you; positively you sha'n't escape.

Enter Crabtree and his precious nephew Sir Benjamin Backbite. There is actually scarcely a brain between them, but Crabtree, prematurely senile, slobbers over the brilliance of the effeminate young dandy who secretly believes himself to be the genius his uncle thinks him.

CRABTREE: Lady Sneerwell, I kiss your hand. Mrs. Candour, I don't believe you are acquainted with my nephew, Sir Benjamin Backbite? Egad, ma'am, he has a pretty wit, and is a pretty poet too; isn't he, Lady Sneerwell?

SIR BENJAMIN: *(with finicking embarrassment)* O fie, uncle!

CRABTREE: *(enthusiastically)* Nay, egad, it's true; I back him at a rebus[8] or a charade against the best rhymer in the kingdom. Has your ladyship heard the epigram he wrote last week on Lady Frizzle's feather catching fire? Do, Benjamin, repeat it, or the charade you made last night extempore at Mrs. Drowzie's conversazione.[9]

---

[8] A puzzle in which pictures represent words.

[9] A social gathering confined to literary and artistic discussion.

Come now; your first is the name of a fish, your second a great naval commander, and—

SIR BENJAMIN: *(overwhelmed at the spectacle of his own genius)* Uncle, now—pr'ythee—

CRABTREE: I'faith, ma'am, 'twould surprise you to hear how ready he is at all these things.

LADY SNEERWELL: *(the cat playing with the mouse)* I wonder, Sir Benjamin, you never publish anything.

SIR BENJAMIN: To say truth, ma'am, 'tis very vulgar to print; and as my little productions are mostly satires and lampoons on particular people, I find they circulate more by giving copies in confidence to the friends of the parties. However, I have some love elegies, which, when favored with this lady's smiles *(bows to Maria),* I mean to give the public.

CRABTREE: *(to Maria)* 'Fore heaven, ma'am, they'll immortalize you! You will be handed down to posterity, like Petrarch's Laura, or Waller's Sacharissa.[10]

SIR BENJAMIN: *(fatuously)* Yes, madam, I think you will like them, when you shall see them on a beautiful quarto page, where a neat rivulet of text shall meander through a meadow of margin. 'Fore Gad, they will be the most elegant things of their kind! *(Maria, embarrassed and justly annoyed, retires with Joseph to the back of the stage where they talk quietly together.)*

CRABTREE: But, ladies, that's true. *(Having done his duty by his nephew, he now turns to a really engrossing topic.)* Have you heard the news?

MRS. CANDOUR: What, sir, do you mean the report of—

CRABTREE: No, ma'am, that's not it. Miss Nicely is going to be married to her own footman.

MRS. CANDOUR: *(joyously)* Impossible!

CRABTREE: *(hurt that his authority is questioned)* Ask Sir Benjamin.

---

[10] Women to whom love poems were addressed by the Italian poet Francesco Petrarca and the British poet Edmund Waller. Sacharissa was Lady Dorothy Sidney.

SIR BENJAMIN: *(eagerly)* 'Tis very true, ma'am; everything is fixed, and the wedding liveries bespoke.

CRABTREE: Yes; and they do say there were *(his tongue lasciviously rolls the "r" as he suppresses a titter)* pressing reasons for it.

LADY SNEERWELL: Why, I have heard something of this before.

MRS. CANDOUR: *(caught in the unusual situation of a defender of reputation)* It can't be, and I wonder anyone should believe such a story, of so prudent a lady as Miss Nicely.

SIR BENJAMIN: Oh, Lud! ma'am, that's the very reason 'twas believed at once. She has always been so cautious and so reserved, that everybody was sure there was some reason for it at the bottom.

MRS. CANDOUR: *(with the mellow knowledge of the family physician)* Why, to be sure, a tale of scandal is as fatal to the credit of a prudent lady of her stamp, as a fever is generally to those of the strongest constitutions. But there is a sort of puny, sickly reputation, that is always ailing, yet will outlive the robuster characters of a hundred prudes.

SIR BENJAMIN: True, madam, there are valetudinarians in reputation as well as constitution; who, being conscious of their weak part, avoid the least breath of air, and supply their want of stamina by care and circumspection.

MRS. CANDOUR: *(still on the defensive)* Well, but this may be all a mistake. You know, Sir Benjamin, very trifling circumstances often give rise to the most injurious tales.

CRABTREE: That they do, I'll be sworn, ma'am. *(relishing a particularly juicy tidbit which has come to his mind)* Did you ever hear how Miss Piper came to lose her lover and her character last summer at Tunbridge? Sir Benjamin, you remember it?

SIR BENJAMIN: *(enthusiastically)* Oh, to be sure! The most whimsical circumstance.

LADY SNEERWELL: *(with poorly suppressed eagerness)* How was it, pray?

CRABTREE: Why, one evening, at Mrs. Ponto's assembly, the conversation happened to turn on the breeding Nova Scotia sheep in this country. Says a young lady in company, "I have known instances of it, for Miss Letitia Piper, a first cousin of mine, had a Nova Scotia sheep that produced her twins." *(dramatically)* "What!" cries the Lady Dowager Dundizzy (who you know is as deaf as a post), "has Miss Piper had twins?" This mistake, as you may imagine, threw the whole company into a fit of laughter. However, 'twas the next morning everywhere reported, and in a few days believed by the whole town, that Miss Letitia Piper had actually been brought to bed of a fine boy and a girl; and in less than a week there were some people who could name the father, and the farm-house where the babies were put to nurse. *(All laugh.)*

LADY SNEERWELL: *(a little skeptical)* Strange, indeed!

CRABTREE: Matter of fact, I assure you. *(struck by another thought, and addressing himself to Joseph)* Oh, Lud! Mr. Surface, pray is it true that your uncle, Sir Oliver, is coming home?

JOSEPH: *(coming forward with Maria)* Not that I know of, indeed, sir.

CRABTREE: He has been in the East Indies a long time. You can scarcely remember him, I believe? *(sighing)* Sad comfort, whenever he returns, to hear how your brother has gone on!

JOSEPH: *(piously as he attacks discreetly what he is pretending to defend)* Charles has been imprudent, sir, to be sure; but I hope no busy people have already prejudiced Sir Oliver against him. He may reform.

SIR BENJAMIN: *(ironically)* To be sure, he may; for my part, I never believed him to be so utterly void of principle as people say; and though he has lost all his friends, I am told nobody is better spoken of by the Jews.

CRABTREE: *(with heavy sarcasm)* That's true, egad,

nephew. If the Old Jewry was a ward, I believe Charles would be an alderman. No man more popular there, 'fore Gad! I hear he pays as many annuities as the Irish tontine;[11] and that whenever he is sick, they have prayers for the recovery of his health in all the synagogues.

SIR BENJAMIN: *(piling it on)* Yet no man lives in greater splendor. They tell me, when he entertains his friends, he will sit down to dinner with a dozen of his own securities; have a score of tradesmen waiting in the antechamber, and an officer behind every guest's chair.

JOSEPH: *(with an eye on Maria and every pretense of brotherly feeling)* This may be entertainment to you, gentlemen, but you pay very little regard to the feelings of a brother.

MARIA: *(aside to the audience)* Their malice is intolerable. *(unable to bear any more)*—Lady Sneerwell, I must wish you a good morning: I'm not very well. *(She leaves hastily through the entrance at the left.)*

MRS. CANDOUR: Oh, dear! she changes color very much.

LADY SNEERWELL: Do, Mrs. Candour, follow her: she may want assistance.

MRS. CANDOUR: That I will, with all my soul, ma'am. Poor dear girl, *(scenting new scandal)* who knows what her situation may be! *(She bustles happily off after Maria.)*

LADY SNEERWELL: 'Twas nothing but that she could not bear to hear Charles reflected on, notwithstanding their difference.

SIR BENJAMIN: *(gloomily)* The young lady's *penchant* is obvious.

CRABTREE: But, Benjamin, you must not give up the pursuit for that: follow her, and put her into good humor. Repeat her some of your own verses. Come, I'll assist you.

---

[11] A scheme for gambling on one's life-expectancy: a number of subscribers contribute to a fund which, with interest, is paid to the last survivor.

SIR BENJAMIN: *(approaching Joseph in a confidential manner)* Mr. Surface, I did not mean to hurt you; but depend on't your brother is utterly undone.

CRABTREE: *(shadowing Sir Benjamin and vastly enjoying the subject)* Oh, Lud, ay! undone as ever man was. Can't raise a guinea! *(He links arms with Sir Benjamin.)*

SIR BENJAMIN: And everything sold, I'm told, that was movable.

CRABTREE: I have seen one that was at his house. Not a thing left but some empty bottles that were overlooked, and the family pictures, which I believe are framed in the wainscots.

SIR BENJAMIN: And I'm very sorry, also, to hear some bad stories against him.

CRABTREE: Oh! he has done many mean things, that's certain. *(He does not elaborate on the "mean things" because he has become suddenly conscious of his hostess' displeasure which he attributes to Joseph's presence. With a trace of awkwardness he bows as a token of leave-taking and backs toward the door, indicating to his nephew that it is time for them to depart.)*

SIR BENJAMIN: *(taking the hint and bowing)* But, however, as he's your brother—*(joining his uncle on the way out)*

CRABTREE: *(hastily, as they make a rather unceremonious departure)* We'll tell you all another opportunity.

LADY SNEERWELL: *(with contemptuous laughter)* Ha! ha! 'tis very hard for them to leave a subject they have not quite run down.

JOSEPH: *(teasingly)* And I believe the abuse was no more acceptable to your ladyship than to Maria.

LADY SNEERWELL: I doubt[12] her affections are farther engaged than we imagined. But the family are to be here this evening, so you may well dine where you are, and we shall have an opportunity of observing farther;

_____
[12] I'm afraid.

(She makes ready to leave.) in the meantime, I'll go and plot mischief, *(amused)* and you shall study sentiment. *(He follows her out of the boudoir to the right.)*

Scene Two

A chamber in Sir Peter Teazle's mansion. Sir Peter, close friend and contemporary of Sir Oliver Surface, is a comically pathetic figure. For years a confirmed bachelor, he has recently married a young and extremely pretty country girl who fascinates and delights him, but who is also thoroughly exasperating in her refusal to take anything seriously, including both his love and his elevation of her from obscurity to a position in high society. Women have always been the particular bane of his existence: he cannot abide their gossiping, and he is extremely disturbed by the undisguised love of his ward Maria for the wastrel Charles. His adoration of Lady Teazle adds to his sense of being a helpless victim. Besides, he is faintly aware that his small and frail frame and spindly shanks (emphasized by his white silk stockings) make him a rather ridiculous looking mate for his vivacious young bride. As the scene begins, he strides in from the right, mumbling irritably to himself.

SIR PETER: When an old bachelor marries a young wife, what is he to expect? 'Tis now six months since Lady Teazle made me the happiest of men; and I have been the most miserable dog ever since! *(reminiscing)* We tifted a little going to church, and fairly quarreled before the bells had done ringing. I was more than once nearly choked with gall during the honeymoon, and had lost all comfort in life before my friends had done wishing me joy. *(deeply puzzled)* Yet I chose with caution— a girl bred wholly in the country, who never knew luxury beyond one silk gown, nor dissipation above the annual gala of a race ball. Yet now she plays her part in all the extravagant fopperies of the fashion and the town, with as ready a grace as if she had never seen a bush or a grass-plot out of Grosvenor Square! I am sneered at by all my acquaintance, and paragraphed in the newspapers. She dissipates my fortune, and contradicts all my humors: yet the worst of it is, I doubt I love her, or I should never bear all this. *(with resolution)* However, I'll never be weak enough to own it.

His soliloquy is interrupted by the entrance from the left of Rowley, sober in dress as he is honest in disposition. The perfect type of the loyal family servant, he was formerly the trusted steward of the father of Joseph and Charles and continues to follow his former patron's affairs with deep concern.

ROWLEY: Oh! Sir Peter, your servant *(bowing);* how is it with you, sir?

SIR PETER: Very bad, Master Rowley, very bad. I meet with nothing but crosses and vexations.

ROWLEY: What can have happened to trouble you since yesterday?

SIR PETER: *(sardonically)* A good question to a married man!

ROWLEY: *(politely)* Nay, I'm sure your lady, Sir Peter, can't be the cause of your uneasiness.

SIR PETER: *(sharply)* Why, has anybody told you she was dead?

ROWLEY: *(rallying him)* Come, come, Sir Peter, you love her, notwithstanding your tempers don't exactly agree.

SIR PETER: *(revealing the flexible disposition of the self-centered bachelor-husband)* But the fault is entirely hers, Master Rowley. I am, myself, the sweetest tempered man alive, and hate a teasing temper; and so I tell her a hundred times a day.

ROWLEY: *(loyally but noncomitally)* Indeed!

SIR PETER: *(earnestly confiding)* Ay; and what is very extraordinary, in all our disputes she is always in the wrong! But Lady Sneerwell, and the set she meets at her house, encourage the perverseness of her disposition. Then, to complete my vexation, Maria, my ward, whom I ought to have the power over, is determined to turn rebel too, and absolutely refuses the man whom I have long resolved on for her husband; meaning, I suppose, to bestow herself on his profligate brother.

ROWLEY: *(earnestly and with freedom of the old family servant)* You know, Sir Peter, I have always taken the liberty to differ with you on the subject of these two young gentlemen. I only wish you may not be deceived in your opinion of the elder. *(with great conviction)* For Charles, my life on't! he will retrieve his errors yet. Their worthy father, once my honored master, was, at his years, nearly as wild a spark; yet, when he died, he did not leave a more benevolent heart to lament his loss.

SIR PETER: *(correcting what he believes to be a mistaken impression)* You are wrong, Master Rowley. On their father's death, you know, I acted as a kind of guardian to them both, till their uncle Sir Oliver's liberality gave them an early independence: of course, no person could have more opportunities of judging of their hearts, and I was never mistaken in my life. *(vehemently)* Joseph is indeed a model for the young men of the age. He is a man of sentiment, and acts up to the sentiments he professes; but for the other, take my word for't, if he had any grain of virtue by descent, he has dissipated it with the rest of his inheritance. Ah! my old friend, Sir Oliver, will be deeply mortified when he finds how part of his bounty has been misapplied.

ROWLEY: *(gently reproving)* I am sorry to find you so violent against the young man, because this may be the critical period of his fortune. I came hither with news that will surprise you.

SIR PETER: *(curious)* What! let me hear.

ROWLEY: Sir Oliver *is* arrived, and at this moment in town.

SIR PETER: *(incredulous)* How! you astonish me! I though you did not expect him this month.

ROWLEY: I did not; but his passage has been remarkably quick.

SIR PETER: *(exhibiting great pleasure)* Egad, I shall rejoice to see my old friend. 'Tis fifteen years since we met. We have had many a day together; *(suddenly re-membering the problem of the two brothers)* but does he still enjoin us not to inform his nephews of his arrival?

ROWLEY: Most strictly. *(explaining)* He means, before it is known, to make some trial of their dispositions.

SIR PETER: *(a bit testily)* Ah! there needs no art to discover their merits; however, he shall have his way. *(defensively and a bit anxiously)* But, pray, does he know I am married?

ROWLEY: *(an imperturable mask-like expression hiding his amusement)* Yes, and will soon wish you joy.

SIR PETER: *(his face clouding)* What, as we drink health to a friend in a consumption. Ah! Oliver will laugh at me. We used to rail at matrimony together, and he has been steady to his text. Well, he must soon be at my house, though! I'll instantly give orders for his reception. *(beseechingly)* But, Master Rowley, don't drop a word that Lady Teazle and I ever disagree.

ROWLEY: *(agreeably)* By no means.

SIR PETER: *(glumly conscious of his quick temper)* For I should never be able to stand Noll's jokes; so I'd have him think, Lord forgive me! that we are a very happy couple.

ROWLEY: I understand you; *(giving warning)* but then you must be very careful not to differ while he is in the house with you.

SIR PETER: *(with sharp realization of his plight)* Egad, and so we must, and that's impossible. *(taking Rowley familiarly by the arm to usher him out)* Ah! Master Rowley, when an old bachelor marries a young wife, he deserves—no—the crime carries its punishment along with it.

He sees Rowley out to the left and, shaking his head ruefully, retires offstage to the right.

ACT TWO

Scene One

A room in Sir Peter's house, one of the many casual rooms typical of the large establishments of the eighteenth century. Sir Peter and his wife enter from the right. He has sought out his wife to make an ultimate attempt to subdue her in anticipation of his old friend's arrival. This battle in the War of the Sexes opens with an uneven distribution of weapons: Lady Teazle's youth, beauty, and vivacious gaiety against Sir Peter's aged stolidity (his port-crimsoned complexion suggesting threatened apoplexy) and his crochety sobriety.

SIR PETER: *(remonstrating with her as they enter together)* Lady Teazle, Lady Teazle, I'll not bear it!

LADY TEAZLE: *(mocking his aging schoolmasterish manner with her habitual light-hearted insouciance)* Sir Peter, Sir Peter, you may bear it or not, as you please; but I ought to have my own way in everything, and what's more, I will, too. What! though I was educated in the country, I know very well that women of fashion are accountable to nobody after they are married.

SIR PETER: *(with heavy sarcasm)* Very well, ma'am, very well; so a husband is to have no influence, no authority?

LADY TEAZLE: *(laughing gaily)* Authority! No, to be sure, if you wanted authority over me, you should have adopted me, and not married me: *(delighting in her strategic advantage)* I am sure you were old enough.

SIR PETER: *(stung to the quick)* Old enough! ay, there it is. *(somewhat subdued and deeply hurt, but determined)* Well, well, Lady Teazle, though my life may be made unhappy by your temper, I'll not be ruined by your extravagance.

LADY TEAZLE: *(with apparently completely honest resentment of a totally undeserved reprimand)* My extravagance! I'm sure I'm not more extravagant than a woman of fashion ought to be.

SIR PETER: *(ignoring her disclaimer)* No, no, madam, you shall throw away no more sums on such unmeaning luxury. *(resuming his tone of angry outrage)* 'Slife! to spend as much to furnish your dressing-room with flowers in winter as would suffice to turn the Pantheon[1] into a green-house, and give a *fête champêtre*[2] at Christmas.

LADY TEAZLE: *(aggrieved at his illogicality)* Am I to blame, Sir Peter, because flowers are dear in cold weather? You should find fault with the climate, and not with me. *(with bland infuriating innocence)* For my part, I'm sure, I wish it was spring all the year round, and that roses grew under our feet. *(She tiptoes across in front of him as if daintily stepping amid roses.)*

SIR PETER: *(raging)* Oons! madam; if you had been born to this, I shouldn't wonder at your talking thus; but you forget what your situation was when I married you.

LADY TEAZLE: *(painfully frank and cheerfully bright in tone)* No, no, I don't; 'twas a very disagreeable one, or I should never have married you.

SIR PETER: *(scarcely hearing her in his intentness on reviving the memory of her previous humble state)* Yes, yes, madam; you were then in a somewhat humbler style: the daughter of a plain country squire. Recollect, Lady Teazle, when I saw you first sitting at your tambor,[3] in a pretty figured linen gown, with a bunch of keys at your side; your hair combed smooth over a roll, and your apartment hung round with fruits in worsted, of your own working.

---

[1] A large London concert hall.
[2] Garden party.
[3] Embroidery frame.

LADY TEAZLE: *(maddeningly agreeable)* Oh, yes! I remember it very well, and a curious life I led—my daily occupation to inspect the dairy, superintend the poultry, make extracts from the family receipt book, and comb my aunt Deborah's lap-dog.

SIR PETER: *(ponderously and a little perplexed at her easy confession)* Yes, yes, ma'am, 'twas so indeed.

LADY TEAZLE: *(prattling on and evidently enjoying a memory that was to have humbled her)* And then, you know, my evening amusements! To draw patterns for ruffles, which I had not materials to make up; to play Pope Joan[4] with the curate; to read a sermon to my aunt; or to be stuck down to an old spinet to strum my father to sleep after a fox-chase. *(She recrosses in front of him, hands outstretched as if about to touch the keys of a spinet.)*

SIR PETER: *(faintly, realizing that he has lost the initiative)* I am glad you have so good a memory. Yes, madam, these were the recreations I took you from; but now you must have your coach—*vis-a-vis*[5]—and three powdered footmen before your chair; and in the summer, a pair of white cats[6] to draw you to Kensington Gardens. No recollection, I suppose, when you were content to ride double, behind the butler, on a docked coach-horse?

LADY TEAZLE: *(in the same tone of conversational cheerfulness)* No; I swear I never did that. I deny the butler and the coach-horse.

SIR PETER: *(emphatically and desperate that he cannot upset Lady Teazle's blithe poise)* This, madam, was your situation; and what have I done for you? I have made you a woman of fashion, of fortune, of rank; in short, I have made you my wife. *(He prances in front of her to the other side, in imitation of her previous maneuvers.)*

LADY TEAZLE: *(her face radiant with a sudden amusing thought as she observes his fragile steps)* Well, then,

---

[4] An unexciting card game.

[5] The most elegant type, with seats facing each other.

[6] Specially bred horses.

and there is but one thing more you can make me to add to the obligation, and that is—

SIR PETER: *(quickly)* My widow, I suppose?

LADY TEAZLE: *(looking down demurely and clearing her throat in a manner that does not at all imply disagreement)* Hem! hem!

SIR PETER: *(coldly and with pompous dignity)* I thank you, madam; but don't flatter yourself; for though your ill conduct may disturb my peace, it shall never break my heart, I promise you; however, I am equally obliged to you for the hint.

LADY TEAZLE: *(petulantly as though talking to a retarded and obstinate child)* Then why will you endeavor to make yourself so disagreeable to me, and thwart me in every little elegant expense?

SIR PETER: *(repeating himself heavily because he can scarcely contain himself.)* 'Slife, madam, I say, had you any of these little elegant expenses when you married me?

LADY TEAZLE: *(gently chiding)* Lud, Sir Peter! would you have me be out of fashion?

SIR PETER: The fashion, indeed! what had you to do with the fashion before you married me?

LADY TEAZLE: For my part, I should think you would like to have your wife thought a woman of taste.

SIR PETER: *(roaring)* Ay, there again; taste! Zounds! madam, you had no taste when you married me!

LADY TEAZLE: *(laughing heartily at him)* That's very true indeed, Sir Peter; and after having married you, I should never pretend to taste again, I allow. *(with a quick change of tone implying "enough of this")* But now, Sir Peter, if we have finished our daily jangle, I presume I may go to my engagement at Lady Sneerwell's.

SIR PETER: *(sourly)* Ah, there's another precious circumstance; a charming set of acquaintance you have made there!

LADY TEAZLE: *(setting him to rights)* Nay, Sir Peter, they are all people of rank and fortune, and remarkably tenacious of reputation.

SIR PETER: *(exhausted but unwilling to forego ex-*

pression of his disgust) Yes, egad, they are tenacious of reputation with a vengeance; for they don't choose anybody should have a character but themselves! Such a crew! Ah! many a wretch has rid on a hurdle[7] who has done less mischief than these utterers of forged tales, coiners of scandal, and clippers of reputation.

LADY TEAZLE: *(archly pretending to high-mindedness)* What! Would you restrain the freedom of speech?

SIR PETER: *(with sorrow and a touch of weariness)* Ah! they have made you just as bad as any one of the society.

LADY TEAZLE: *(more pleased than contrite)* Why, I believe I do bear a part with a tolerable grace. But I vow I bear no malice against the people I abuse. When I say an ill-natured thing, 'tis out of pure good humor; and I take it for granted, they deal exactly in the same manner with me. *(preparing to take her departure)* But, Sir Peter, you know you promised to come to Lady Sneerwell's too.

SIR PETER: Well, well, I'll call in just to look after my own character.

LADY TEAZLE: Then indeed you must make haste after me, or you'll be too late. *(with affectionate cheerfulness)* So, good-bye to ye. *(She glides out to the left.)*

SIR PETER: *(impressed by his own futile exertions and bowing to the mystery of the eternal feminine)* So, I have gained much by my intended expostulation; yet, with what a charming air she contradicts everything I say, and how pleasingly she shows her contempt for my authority! Well, though I can't make her love me, there is great satisfaction in quarreling with her; and I think she never appears to such advantage as when she is doing everything in her power to plague me. *(He goes off to the right, meditatively shaking his head.)*

Scene Two

The clique has assembled again at Lady Sneerwell's. They come drifting in from another part of the house at

---

[7] Cart carrying prisoners to the gallows.

the right into an elaborately decorated parlor. They are continuing a stream of conversation which originated elsewhere, probably at dinner. A card table at the left, with cards scattered on it, suggests that a game was in progress at an earlier time. Lady Sneerwell and Joseph lead the way, followed by Mrs. Candour attended by the inseparable Crabtree and Sir Benjamin Backbite.

LADY SNEERWELL: *(turning to Sir Benjamin and tapping him playfully with her fan)* Nay, positively, we will hear it.

JOSEPH: *(completely in character)* Yes, yes, the epigram by all means.

SIR BENJAMIN: *(wanting to be urged)* Oh, plague on't, uncle! 'tis mere nonsense.

CRABTREE: No, no; 'fore Gad, very clever for an extempore!

SIR BENJAMIN: *(in fatuous surrender to the demands of his public)* But, ladies, you should be acquainted with the circumstances. You must know, that one day last week, as Lady Betty Curricle was taking the dust in Hyde Park, in a sort of duodecimo phaeton,[1] she desired me to write some verses on her ponies, upon which I took out my pocketbook, and in one moment produced the following:

Sure never were seen two such beautiful ponies;
Other horses are clowns, but these macaronies:
To give them this title I'm sure can't be wrong,
Their legs are so slim, and their tails are so long.

CRABTREE: *(Never getting over his amazement at his nephew's cleverness)* There, ladies, done in the smack of a whip, and on horseback too.

JOSEPH: A very Phoebus[2] mounted, indeed, Sir Benjamin. *(bowing in tribute)*

SIR BENJAMIN: *(with airy modesty and a wave of his*

---

[1] He is being devastatingly clever in his reference to the smallness of her carriage and the consequent discomfort of being so close to the dirt of this most fashionable and heavily trafficked drive. A book in duodecimo is pocket size.

[2] Apollo, god of poetry.

kerchief) Oh, dear sir! trifles, trifles.

*The entrance from the left of Lady Teazle and Maria
at this point occasions no especial notice by the others.
It is not surprising that the two younger women have
been drawn together since neither one has the hardened
callousness of the charter members of the clique. Only
Joseph bows as they enter and joins them.*

MRS. CANDOUR: I must have a copy.

LADY SNEERWELL: *(always the good hostess)* Lady
Teazle, I hope we shall see Sir Peter?

LADY TEAZLE: I believe he'll wait on your ladyship
presently.

LADY SNEERWELL: Maria, my love, you look grave.
(tactfully maneuvering her for Joseph's sake) Come, you
shall sit down to piquet[3] with Mr. Surface.

MARIA: *(meekly)* I take very little pleasure in cards;
however, I'll do as you please. *(She sits down at the card
table opposite Joseph; they begin to play.)*

LADY TEAZLE: *(aside, puzzled, ingenuously unaware of
Joseph's real interests)* I am surprised Mr. Surface should
sit down with her; I thought he would have embraced
this opportunity of speaking to me, before Sir Peter came.

MRS. CANDOUR: *(continuing the general conversation
which has proceeded without notice of the quiet maneuvering of Lady Sneerwell)* Now, I'll die, but you are
so scandalous, I'll forswear your society.

LADY TEAZLE: *(only momentarily upset by having
been prevented from continuing an amusing flirtation
with Joseph)* What's the matter, Mrs. Candour?

MRS. CANDOUR: *(including her in the circle)* They'll
not allow our friend, Miss Vermilion, to be handsome.

LADY SNEERWELL: Oh, surely she is a pretty woman.

CRABTREE: *(without conviction)* I'm very glad you
think so, ma'am.

MRS. CANDOUR: She has a charming fresh color.

LADY TEAZLE: *(particularly enjoying an opportunity
to be malicious to relieve her slightly piqued feelings)*
Yes, when it is fresh put on.

---

[3] A card game for two players.

MRS. CANDOUR: Oh, fie! I'll swear her color is natural; I have seen it come and go.

LADY TEAZLE: I dare swear you have, ma'am; it goes off at night, and comes again in the morning.

SIR BENJAMIN: *(heavily pursuing the obvious)* True, ma'am, it not only comes and goes, but what's more, egad! her maid can fetch and carry it. *(They all laugh.)*

MRS. CANDOUR: Ha! ha! ha! how I hate to hear you talk so! But surely, now, her sister *is,* or *was,* very handsome.

CRABTREE: Who? Mrs. Evergreen? Oh, Lord, she's six and fifty if she's an hour.

MRS. CANDOUR: Now positively you wrong her; fifty-two or fifty-three is the utmost; and I don't think she looks more.

SIR BENJAMIN: Ah! there's no judging by her looks, unless one could see her face.

LADY SNEERWELL: *(living up to her name)* Well, well, if Mrs. Evergreen *does* take some pains to repair the ravages of time, you must allow she effects it with great ingenuity, and surely that's better than the careless manner in which the widow Ochre chalks her wrinkles.

SIR BENJAMIN: Nay, now, Lady Sneerwell, you are severe upon the widow. Come, come, 'tis not that she paints so ill, but when she has finished her face, she joins it so badly to her neck, that she looks like a mended statue, in which the connoisseur sees at once that the head's modern though the trunk's antique.

CRABTREE: *(genuinely surprised at his nephew's accidental brilliance)* Ha! ha! ha! well said, nephew.

MRS. CANDOUR: Ha! ha! ha! well, you make me laugh, but I vow I hate you for it. What do you think of Miss Simper?

SIR BENJAMIN: Why, she has very pretty teeth.

LADY TEAZLE: *(vivaciously enjoying the mischief)* Yes, and on that account, when she is neither speaking nor laughing (which very seldom happens), she never abso lutely shuts her mouth, but leaves it on a jar, as it were—thus—*(opens her mouth in a simpering grimace which fully reveals her teeth, while mumbling "your most obedient.")*

MRS. CANDOUR: *(no more really serious than previously in her objections)* How can you be so ill-natured?

LADY TEAZLE: *(encouraged)* Nay, I allow even that's better than the pains Mrs. Prim takes to conceal her losses in front. She draws her mouth till it positively resembles the aperture of a poor's box,[4] and all her words appear to slide out edgewise, as it were thus, *(with barely opened lips) How do you do, madam? Yes, madam.*

LADY SNEERWELL: *(approving)* Very well, Lady Teazle; I see you can be a little severe.

LADY TEAZLE: In defense of a friend it is but justice. *(becoming suddenly grave as she catches sight of her husband as he is about to enter from the left)* But here comes Sir Peter to spoil our pleasantry.

Sir Peter enters, including the whole company in a sweeping bow.

SIR PETER: Ladies, your most obedient. *(aside)* Mercy on me! here is the whole set! a character dead at every word, I suppose. *(He remains somewhat remote from the others and occasionally raises his lorgnette to his eye as if unable to quite credit what he sees.)*

MRS. CANDOUR: *(gushing)* I am rejoiced you are come, Sir Peter. They have been *so* censorious; and Lady Teazle as bad as anyone.

SIR PETER: *(with only the most barely perceptible touch of sarcasm)* It must be very distressing to *you*, Mrs. Candour, I dare swear.

MRS. CANDOUR: *(blissfully unconscious of the innuendo)* Oh, they will allow good qualities to nobody; not even good nature to our friend Mrs. Pursy.

LADY TEAZLE: What, the fat dowager who was at Mrs. Quadrille's last night?

MRS. CANDOUR: Nay, her bulk is her misfortune; and when she takes such pains to get rid of it, you ought not to reflect on her.

---

4 Box placed at the rear of a church with a narrow slit to receive offerings for the poor.

LADY SNEERWELL: That's very true, indeed.

LADY TEAZLE: Yes, I know she almost lives on acids and small whey; laces herself by pulleys; and often, in the hottest noon in summer, you may see her on a little squat pony, with her hair plaited up behind like a drummer's, and puffing round the Ring[5] on a full trot. *(They all laugh.)*

MRS. CANDOUR: I thank you, Lady Teazle, for defending her.

SIR PETER: *(with heavy sarcasm)* Yes, a good defense, truly!

MRS. CANDOUR: Truly, Lady Teazle is as censorious as Miss Sallow.

CRABTREE: *(quite oblivious to a perfect description of himself)* Yes, and she is a curious being to pretend to be censorious—an awkward gawky, without any one good point under heaven.

MRS. CANDOUR: *(clinging to her one tactic of malice)* Positively you shall not be so very severe. Miss Sallow is a near relation of mine by marriage, and as for her person, great allowance is to be made; for, let me tell you, a woman labors under many disadvantages who tries to pass for a girl at six-and-thirty.

LADY SNEERWELL: Though, surely, she is handsome still; *(continuing the game of damning by defending)* and for the weakness in her eyes, considering how much she reads by candlelight, it is not to be wondered at.

MRS. CANDOUR: *(really warming to the subject)* True, and then as to her manner; upon my word I think it is particularly graceful, considering she never had the least education; for you know her mother was a Welsh milliner, and her father a sugar-baker at Bristol.

SIR BENJAMIN: *(laughing)* Ah, you are both of you too good natured!

SIR PETER: *(aside, truly scandalized)* Yes, damned good natured! This their own relation! mercy on me!

MRS. CANDOUR: *(probably completely unconscious of*

---

5 The circular drive in Hyde Park.

her own hypocrisy) For my own part, I own I cannot bear to hear a friend ill spoken of.

SIR PETER: *(with obvious disgust)* No, to be sure!

SIR BENJAMIN: *(to Sir Peter with a touch of malicious teasing)* Oh! you are of a moral turn. Mrs. Candour and I can sit for an hour and hear Lady Stucco talk sentiment.

LADY TEAZLE: Nay, I vow Lady Stucco is very well with the dessert after dinner; for she's just like the French fruits one cracks for mottoes[6]—made up of paint and proverb.

MRS. CANDOUR: *(tirelessly)* Well, I never will join you in ridiculing a friend; and so I constantly tell my cousin Ogle, and you all know what pretensions she has to be critical on beauty.

CRABTREE: Oh, to be sure! she has herself the oddest countenance that ever was seen; 'tis a collection of features from all the different countries of the globe.

SIR BENJAMIN: So she has, indeed—an Irish front—

CRABTREE: Caledonian locks—

SIR BENJAMIN: Dutch nose—

CRABTREE: Austrian lips—

SIR BENJAMIN: Complexion of a Spaniard—

CRABTREE: And teeth *a la Chinois*.[7]

SIR BENJAMIN: In short, her face resembles a *table d'hote* at Spa,[8] where no two guests are of a nation—

CRABTREE: *(radiantly determined to trump all the cards)* Or a congress at the close of a general war—wherein all the members, even to her eyes, appear to have a different interest, and her nose and chin are the only parties likely to join issue. *(There is general laughter; Sir Peter shakes his head in mournful wonderment.)*

MRS. CANDOUR: Ha! ha! ha! *(louder than the others)*

---

[6] Proverbs and wise sayings on printed slips of paper inserted inside the confections.

[7] Chinese.

[8] A famous international resort in Belgium.

SIR PETER: *(aside)* Mercy on my life!—a person they dine with twice a week.

LADY SNEERWELL: Go, go; you are a couple of provoking toads.

MRS. CANDOUR: Nay, but I vow you shall not carry the laugh off so; for give me leave to say that Mrs. Ogle—

SIR PETER: *(unable to stand any more, coming forward and addressing Mrs. Candour)* Madam, madam, I beg your pardon; there's no stopping these good gentlemen's tongues. But when I tell you, Mrs. Candour, that the lady they are abusing is a particular friend of mine, I hope you'll not take her part.

LADY SNEERWELL: *(contemptuous of one who prefers good manners to good malice)* Ha! ha! ha! Well said, Sir Peter! But you are a cruel creature—too phlegmatic yourself for a jest, and too peevish to allow wit in others.

SIR PETER: *(seriously)* Ah, madam, true wit is more nearly allied to good nature than your ladyship is aware of.

LADY TEAZLE: *(walking up to him and tapping him condescendingly on the shoulder with her fan with heartless innuendo)* True, Sir Peter. I believe they are so near akin that they can never be united.

SIR BENJAMIN: *(superciliously delighted at catching her implied reference to her own marriage)* Or rather, madam, suppose them to be man and wife, because one seldom sees them together.

LADY TEAZLE: *(deliberately continuing her outrageous teasing)* But Sir Peter is such an enemy to scandal, I believe he would have it put down by Parliament.

SIR PETER: *(vehement as always when turned on by his wife)* 'Fore heaven, madam, if they were to consider the sporting with reputation of as much importance as poaching on manors, and pass an Act for the Preservation of Fame, I believe there are many would thank them for the bill.

LADY SNEERWELL: Oh, Lud! Sir Peter; would you deprive us of our privileges?

SIR PETER: *(aroused to the point of being really cutting)* Ay, madam; and then no person should be permitted to kill characters or run down reputations, but qualified old maids and disappointed widows.

LADY SNEERWELL: *(left without effective retort to this unexpected reference to her widowhood)* Go, you monster!

MRS. CANDOUR: *(attempting to moderate the discussion)* But, surely, you would not be quite so severe on those who only report what they hear?

SIR PETER: *(his indignation stimulating him to eloquence)* Yes, madam, I would have law merchant[9] for them too; and in all cases of slander currency, whenever the drawer of the lie was not to be found, the injured parties should have a right to come on any of the indorsers.

CRABTREE: *(with belated and prissy righteousness)* Well, for my part, I believe there never was a scandalous tale without some foundation.

SIR PETER: Oh, nine out of ten of the malicious inventions are founded on some ridiculous misrepresentation.

LADY SNEERWELL: *(determined to bring a halt to this unpleasant argument)* Come, ladies, shall we sit down to cards in the next room?

During this speech a servant enters from the left and whispers a message to Sir Peter.

SIR PETER: *(to the servant)* I'll be with them directly. *(aside, as the servant exits)* I'll get away unperceived.

LADY SNEERWELL: *(aware of his intention, with acid politeness)* Sir Peter, you are not going to leave us?

SIR PETER: Your ladyship must excuse me; I'm called away by particular business. *(taking his leave with a Parthian shot)* But I leave my character behind me. *(He goes off to the left.)*

SIR BENJAMIN: Well certainly, Lady Teazle, that lord

---

[9] Commercial law by which endorsers of notes are responsible on default of the makers.

of yours is a strange being; I could tell you some stories of him would make you laugh heartily if he were not your husband.

LADY TEAZLE: *(merrily)* Oh, pray don't mind that; come do let's hear them.

During these last lines Lady Sneerwell has been moving with her guests toward the card room at the right. Lady Teazle is the last to go, leaving Joseph and Maria alone at their card game. Joseph, carefully observing their departure, puts down his cards, takes Maria by the hand, and leads her gently toward the front of the stage.

JOSEPH: *(with pretended sympathy)* Maria, I see you have no satisfaction in this society.

MARIA: *(with real distress)* How is it possible I should? If to raise malicious smiles at the infirmities or misfortunes of those who have never injured us be the province of wit or humor, Heaven grant me a double portion of dullness!

JOSEPH: *(in kindly explanation of this naïve girl while attempting to rationalize his own participation in this company)* Yet they appear more ill-natured than they are; they have no malice at heart.

MARIA: *(with rising fervor because she is not susceptible to instruction of this sort)* Then is their conduct still more contemptible; for, in my opinion, nothing could excuse the intemperance of their tongues, but a natural and uncontrollable bitterness of mind.

JOSEPH: *(concluding by her heated tone that she is not to be converted; hence a quick and quiet reversal of tone)* Undoubtedly, madam; and it has always been a sentiment of mine, that to propagate a malicious truth wantonly is more despicable than to falsify from revenge. *(suddenly shifting to a pleading tone)* But can you, Maria, feel thus for others, and be unkind to me alone? Is hope to be denied the tenderest passion?

MARIA: *(very uncomfortable)* Why will you distress me by renewing this subject?

JOSEPH: *(assuming a tragic manner)* Ah, Maria! you would not treat me thus, and oppose your guardian, Sir

Peter's will, but that I see that profligate Charles is still a favored rival.

MARIA: *(angrily)* Ungenerously urged! But whatever my sentiments are for that unfortunate young man, be assured I shall not feel more bound to give him up, because his distresses have lost him the regard even of a brother.

JOSEPH: *(in a frantic attempt to regain lost ground)* Nay, but Maria, do not leave me with a frown; *(kneeling at her feet)* by all that's honest, I swear—*(aside, as he catches sight of Lady Teazle about to put in an unexpected appearance)* Gad's life, here's Lady Teazle! *(continuing, to Maria)* You must not—no, you shall not —for, though I have the greatest regard for Lady Teazle—

MARIA: *(completely bewildered)* Lady Teazle!

JOSEPH: Yet were Sir Peter to suspect—

LADY TEAZLE: *(entering)* What is this, pray? Do you take her for me? Child, you are wanted in the next room. *(Maria slides out in embarrassment as Lady Teazle confronts her presumed ardent admirer)* What is all this, pray? *(Joseph rises to his feet.)*

JOSEPH: *(glibly)* Oh, the most unlucky circumstance in nature! Maria has somehow suspected the tender concern I have for your happiness, and threatened to acquaint Sir Peter with her suspicions, and I was just endeavoring to reason with her when you came in.

LADY TEAZLE: *(highly skeptical)* Indeed! but you seemed to adopt a very tender mode of reasoning. Do you usually argue on your knees?

JOSEPH: *(with easy self-possession)* Oh, she's a child, and I thought a little bombast—*(cleverly turning Lady Teazle's attention to herself)* But, Lady Teazle, when are you to give me your judgment on my library, as you promised?

LADY TEAZLE: *(more impressed by what she has seen than by what Joseph has told her)* No, no; I begin to think it would be imprudent, *(recovering her habitual*

Gad's life, here's Lady Teazle!

aplomb) and you know I admit you as a lover no farther than fashion sanctions.

JOSEPH: *(with dry humor)* True, a mere platonic cicisbeo[10]—what every wife is entitled to.

LADY TEAZLE: Certainly, one must not be out of fashion. However, *(the lady of fashion surrendering to the rural maid)* I have so many of my country prejudices left, that, though Sir Peter's ill-humor may vex me ever so, it never shall provoke me to—

JOSEPH: *(completing the sentence for her)* The only revenge in your power. *(sardonically)* Well, I applaud your moderation.

LADY TEAZLE: *(flirtatiously)* Go; you are an insinuating wretch. But we shall be missed; let us join the company.

JOSEPH: But we had best not return together.

LADY TEAZLE: *(insinuatingly)* Well, don't stay; for Maria sha'n't come to hear any more of your reasoning, I promise you. *(She goes to join the others.)*

JOSEPH: *(alone and deeply troubled)* A curious dilemma my politics have run me into! I wanted, at first, only to ingratiate myself with Lady Teazle, that she might not be my enemy with Maria; and I have, I don't know how, become her serious lover. Sincerely I begin to wish I had never made such a point of gaining so very good a character, for it has led me into so many cursed rogueries that I doubt I shall be exposed at last. *(with which foreboding he also leaves to join the card players.)*

Scene Three

A reception room in Sir Peter Teazle's house. At the opening of the scene, Rowley and Sir Oliver Surface, who have been admitted to call on Sir Peter, enter the room from the left. Sir Oliver, who as an old friend belongs to Sir Peter's generation, is dressed expensively but soberly. Portly in figure and carrying a cane, he

---

[10] Italian term for a gallant of a married woman.

looks and acts like a man who has enjoyed hearty living, can take a joke, and takes a broad view of human idiosyncracies. His travels have robbed him of any provincialism he might have been bred to; he is, in the literal sense of the phrase, a man of the world.

SIR OLIVER: *(a little too robustious)* Ha! ha! ha! So my old friend is married, hey?—a young wife out of the country. Ha! ha! ha! that he should have stood bluff to old bachelor so long, and sink into a husband at last!

ROWLEY: *(alarmed)* But you must not rally him on the subject, Sir Oliver; 'tis a tender point, I assure you, though he has been married only seven months.

SIR OLIVER: *(gustily)* Then he has been just half a year on the stool of repentance! Poor Peter! But you say he has entirely given up Charles—never sees him, hey?

ROWLEY: *(on the defensive)* His prejudice against him is astonishing, and I am sure greatly increased by a jealousy of him with Lady Teazle, which he has industriously been led into by a scandalous society in the neighborhood, who have contributed not a little to Charles's ill name. Whereas the truth is, I believe, if the lady is partial to either of them, his brother is the favorite.

SIR OLIVER: Ay, I know there is a set of malicious, prating, prudent gossips, both male and female, who murder characters to kill time, and will rob a young fellow of his good name before he has years to know the value of it. But I am not to be prejudiced against my nephew by such, I promise you. No, no; if Charles has done nothing false or mean, I shall compound for his extravagance.

ROWLEY: Then, my life on't, you will reclaim him. *(appreciatively)* Ah, sir! it gives me new life to find that *your* heart is not turned against him; and that the son of my good old master has one friend, however, left.

SIR OLIVER: *(with customary generosity)* What! shall I forget, Master Rowley, when I was at his years myself? Egad, my brother and I were neither of us very prudent youths; and yet, I believe, you have not seen many better men than your old master was.

ROWLEY: Sir, 'tis this reflection gives me assurance that Charles may yet be a credit to his family. But here comes Sir Peter.

SIR OLIVER: Egad, so he does. Mercy on me! he's greatly altered, and seems to have a settled married look! One may read *husband* in his face at this distance!

Sir Peter, entering from the right with arms outstretched, comes forward to greet his old friend.

SIR PETER: Ha! Sir Oliver, my old friend! Welcome to England a thousand times!

SIR OLIVER: Thank you—thank you, Sir Peter! and i'faith I am glad to find you well, believe me.

SIR PETER: Oh! 'tis a long time since we met—fifteen years, I doubt, Sir Oliver, and many a cross accident in the time.

SIR OLIVER: Ay, I have had my share. But what! I find you are married, hey? *(as though at a sick-bed)* Well, well, it can't be helped; and so—I wish you joy with all my heart.

SIR PETER: *(bucking up)* Thank you, thank you, Sir Oliver. Yes, I have entered into—*(hesitating)* the happy state; *(quickly)* but we'll not talk of that now.

SIR OLIVER: *(jokingly)* True, true, Sir Peter; old friends should not begin on grievances at first meeting; no, no, no.

ROWLEY: *(under his breath)* Take care, pray, sir.

SIR OLIVER: *(heeding the warning to veer from this delicate topic)* Well, so one of my nephews is a wild fellow, hey?

SIR PETER: *(sorrowfully)* Wild! Ah! my old friend, I grieve for your disappointment there; he's a lost young man, indeed. However, his brother will make you amends. Joseph is, indeed, what a youth should be. Everybody in the world speaks well of him.

SIR OLIVER: *(skeptically)* I am sorry to hear it; he has too good a character to be an honest fellow. Everybody speaks well of him! Pshaw! then he has bowed as low to knaves and fools as to the honest dignity of genius and virtue.

SIR PETER: *(taken aback)* What, Sir Oliver! do you blame him for not making enemies?

SIR OLIVER: *(bluntly)* Yes, if he has merit enough to deserve them.

SIR PETER: Well, well; you'll be convinced when you know him. 'Tis edification to hear him converse; he professes the noblest sentiments.

SIR OLIVER: *(annoyed)* Oh! plague of his sentiments! If he salutes me with a scrap of morality in his mouth, I shall be sick directly *(reconsidering, in fairness, his instinctive outburst)* But, however, don't mistake me, Sir Peter; I don't mean to defend Charles's errors—but before I form my judgment of either of them, I intend to make a trial of their hearts; and my friend Rowley and I have planned something for the purpose.

ROWLEY: *(with conviction)* And Sir Peter shall own for once he has been mistaken.

SIR PETER: *(with equal conviction)* Oh! my life on Joseph's honor.

SIR OLIVER: Well—come, give us a bottle of good wine, and we'll drink the lad's health, and tell you our scheme.

SIR PETER: *Allons,*[1] then!

SIR OLIVER: *(expansively)* And don't, Sir Peter, be so severe against your old friend's son. Odds my life! I am not sorry that he has run out of the course a little; for my part I hate to see prudence clinging to the green suckers of youth; 'tis like ivy round a sapling, and spoils the growth of the tree. *(They all go off together to the right.)*

---

[1] Let us go.

ACT THREE

Scene One

Another room in Sir Peter Teazle's house, presumably his study or library. The three men of the previous scene have repaired here to discuss the scheme just mentioned over the wine Sir Oliver has proposed. Their conversation has continued during their passage from the reception room. They enter the room from the inner or right-hand door.

SIR PETER: Well, then, we will see this fellow first, and have our wine afterwards; but how is this, Master Rowley? I don't see the jet[1] of your scheme.

ROWLEY: Why sir, this Mr. Stanley, whom I was speaking of, is nearly related to them by their mother. He was a merchant in Dublin, but has been ruined by a series of undeserved misfortunes. He has applied, by letter, to Mr. Surface and Charles; from the former he has received nothing but evasive promises of future service, while Charles has done all that his extravagance has left him power to do, and he is, at this time, endeavoring to raise a sum of money, part of which, in the midst of his own distresses, I know he intends for the service of poor Stanley.

SIR OLIVER: *(immensely pleased)* Ah! he is my brother's son.

SIR PETER: *(interested but puzzled)* Well, but how is Sir Oliver personally to—

ROWLEY: *(anticipating his question)* Why, sir, I will inform Charles and his brother that Stanley has obtained permission to apply personally to his friends, and as they

---
[1] Intent, or point.

92

have neither of them ever seen him, let Sir Oliver assume his character, and he will have a fair opportunity of judging, at least, of the benevolence of their dispositions; and believe me, sir, you will find in the younger brother one who, in the midst of folly and dissipation, has still, as our immortal bard expresses it, "a heart to pity, and a hand, open as day, for melting charity."

SIR PETER: *(unimpressed by Rowley's eloquence)* Pshaw! What signifies his having an open hand or purse either, when he has nothing left to give? Well, well, make the trial, if you please. But where is the fellow whom you brought for Sir Oliver to examine, relative to Charles's affairs?

ROWLEY: Below, waiting his commands, and no one can give him better intelligence. This, Sir Oliver, is a friendly Jew, who, to do him justice, has done everything in his power to bring your nephew to a proper sense of his extravagance.

SIR PETER: Pray let us have him in.

ROWLEY: *(to the servant who has been standing ready to serve refreshments when signalled)* Desire Mr. Moses to walk upstairs. *(The servant bows silently and obeys.)*

SIR PETER: *(with continued skepticism)* But, pray, why should you suppose he will speak the truth?

ROWLEY: *(with confidence)* Oh! I have convinced him that he has no chance of recovering certain sums advanced to Charles, but through the bounty of Sir Oliver, who he knows is arrived, so that you may depend on his fidelity to his own interests. I have also another evidence in my power—one Snake, whom I have detected in a matter little short of forgery, and shall speedily produce him to remove some of your prejudices.

SIR PETER: *(recognizing the name of Lady Sneerwell's toady)* I have heard too much on that subject.

ROWLEY: *(in a commendatory manner)* Here comes the honest Israelite. *(beckons Moses, who appears at the door at the left, to enter. Moses is somewhat past middle age; he is soberly dressed as befits his scorned but necessary profession of money-lender. He is re-*

spectful but not servile and bears himself with a kind of innate dignity that bespeaks awareness of the contempt commonly visited upon his class but which, in his own case at least, he knows to be entirely undeserved. He is introduced in a businesslike manner.) This is Sir Oliver.

SIR OLIVER: *(getting to the point at once)* Sir, I understand you have lately had great dealings with my nephew, Charles.

MOSES: *(sincerely)* Yes, Sir Oliver, I have done all I could for him; *(with mournful recollection)* but he was ruined before he came to me for assistance.

SIR OLIVER: *(disdainfully)* That was unlucky, truly; for you have had no opportunity of showing your talents.

MOSES: *(unconsciously betraying the ingrained rapacity of his profession)* None at all; I hadn't the pleasure of knowing his distresses till he was some thousands worse than nothing.

SIR OLIVER: *(vehemently sarcastic)* Unfortunate, indeed! But I suppose you have done all in your power for him, honest Moses?

MOSES: *(ignoring the sarcasm)* Yes, he knows that. This very evening I was to have brought him a gentleman from the city, who does not know him, and will, I believe, advance him some money.

SIR PETER: *(with mock surprise)* What! one Charles has never had money from before?

MOSES: Yes; Mr. Premium of Crutched Friars, formerly a broker.

SIR PETER: *(inspired)* Egad, Sir Oliver, a thought strikes me! Charles, you say, does not know Mr. Premium?

MOSES: Not at all.

SIR PETER: Now then, Sir Oliver, you may have a better opportunity of satisfying yourself than by an old romancing tale of a poor relation. Go with my friend Moses, and represent Premium, and then, I'll answer for it, you'll see your nephew in all his glory.

SIR OLIVER: *(delighted)* Egad, I like this idea better

than the other, and I may visit Joseph afterwards as Old Stanley.

SIR PETER: True, so you may.

ROWLEY: *(not entirely happy about the scheme)* Well, this is taking Charles rather at a disadvantage, to be sure. However, Moses, you understand Sir Peter, and will be faithful?

MOSES: You may depend upon me. *(looking at his watch)* This is near the time I was to have gone.

SIR OLIVER: I'll accompany you as soon as you please, Moses. *(struck by a sudden thought)* But hold! I have forgot one thing—how the plague shall I be able to pass for a Jew?

MOSES: *(revealing that Mr. Premium is a well-to-do gentile)* There's no need—the principal is Christian.

SIR OLIVER: *(surprised)* Is he? I'm very sorry to hear it. But then, again, a'n't I rather too smartly dressed to look like a money lender?

SIR PETER: Not at all; 'twould not be out of character if you went in your own carriage—would it, Moses?

MOSES: Not in the least.

SIR OLIVER: Well, but how must I talk? There's certainly some cant of usury and mode of treating that I ought to know.

SIR PETER: Oh! there's not much to learn. *(with heavy jocularity)* The great point, as I take it, is to be exorbitant enough in your demands—hey, Moses?

MOSES: Yes, that's a very great point.

SIR OLIVER: I'll answer for't I'll not be wanting in that. I'll ask him eight or ten percent on the loan at least.

MOSES: *(sincerely scandalized)* If you ask him no more than that, you'll be discovered immediately.

SIR OLIVER: *(horrified)* Hey! what the plague! How much, then?

MOSES: *(with professional blandness)* That depends upon the circumstances. If he appears not very anxious for the supply, you should require only forty or fifty percent; but if you find him in great distress, and want the moneys very bad, you may ask double.

SIR PETER: *(amused)* A good honest trade you're learning, Sir Oliver!

SIR OLIVER: *(emphatically)* Truly, I think so; and not unprofitable.

MOSES: *(continuing his instructions)* Then, you know, you hav'n't the moneys yourself, but are forced to borrow them for him of an old friend.

SIR OLIVER: Oh! I borrow it of a friend, do I?

MOSES: And your friend is an unconscionable dog; but you can't help that.

SIR OLIVER: *(unable to credit his ears)* My friend is an unconscionable dog?

MOSES: *(ignoring Sir Oliver's shocked exclamation)* Yes, and he himself has not the moneys by him, but is forced to sell stock at a great loss.

SIR OLIVER: *(overwhelmed)* He is forced to sell stock at a great loss, is he? Well, that's very kind of him.

SIR PETER: *(thoroughly enjoying his friend's innocence)* I' faith, Sir Oliver—Mr. Premium, I mean—you'll soon be master of the trade. But, Moses! would not you have him run out a little against the Annuity Bill?[2] That would be in character, I should think.

MOSES: Very much.

ROWLEY: *(entering the fun of this satirical attack)* And lament that a young man now must be at years of discretion before he is suffered to ruin himself?

MOSES: Ay, great pity!

SIR PETER: *(lapsing into Parliamentary oratory)* And abuse the public for allowing merit to an Act, whose only object is to snatch misfortune and imprudence from the rapacious gripe of usury, and give the minor a chance of inheriting his estate without being undone by coming into possession.

SIR OLIVER: *(terminating the discussion)* So, so; Moses shall give me further instructions as we go together.

SIR PETER: You will not have much time, for your nephew lives hard by.

SIR OLIVER: Oh, never fear! My tutor appears so able,

---

[2] A bill, recently passed, to protect the annuities of minors.

that though Charles lived in the next street, it must be
my own fault if I am not a complete rogue before I
turn the corner.

*Sir Oliver and Moses leave together by the left door to
call on Charles. Moses bows low as he departs.*

SIR PETER: *(believing this unexpected turn of affairs
will bring Sir Oliver to agree with his own judgment of
Joseph and Charles)* So now, I think Sir Oliver will be
convinced. You are partial, Rowley, and would have
prepared Charles for the other plot.

ROWLEY: *(protesting)* No, upon my word, Sir Peter.

SIR PETER: Well, go bring me this Snake, and I'll hear
what he has to say presently. *(looks toward the wings at
the left.)* I see Maria, and want to speak with her. *(Rowley leaves as Sir Peter becomes suddenly wrapped in his
own jealous broodings.)* I should be glad to be convinced my suspicions of Lady Teazle and Charles were
unjust. I have never yet opened my mind on this subject
to my friend Joseph. I am determined I will do it; he
will give me his opinion sincerely. *(Maria comes in.)* So,
child, has Mr. Surface returned with you?

MARIA: No, sir; he was engaged.

SIR PETER: *(disappointed but not distracted from pursuing his well-meant supervision of his ward's welfare)*
Well, Maria, do you not reflect, the more you converse
with that amiable young man, what return his partiality
for you deserves?

MARIA: *(fretfully)* Indeed, Sir Peter, your frequent
importunity on this subject distresses me extremely; you
compel me to declare that I know no man who has ever
paid me a particular attention whom I would not prefer
to Mr. Surface.

SIR PETER: *(angered)* So, here's perverseness! No, no,
Maria, 'tis Charles only whom you would prefer. 'Tis
evident his vices and follies have won your heart.

MARIA: *(earnestly)* This is unkind, sir. You know I
have obeyed you in neither seeing nor corresponding
with him. I have heard enough to convince me that he
is unworthy my regard. Yet I cannot think it culpable, if,

while my understanding severely condemns his vices, *(with sudden tremulousness of voice)* my heart suggests some pity for his distresses.

SIR PETER: *(gruffly)* Well, well, pity him as much as you please; but give your heart and hand to a worthier object.

MARIA: *(with determination)* Never to his brother!

SIR PETER: *(furious at his inability to cope with any of the women of his household)* Go, perverse and obstinate! But take care, madam; you have never yet known what the authority of a guardian is. Don't compel me to inform you of it.

MARIA: *(close to tears)* I can only say, you shall not have just reason. 'Tis true, by my father's will, I am for a short period bound to regard you as his substitute; but must cease to think you so, when you would compel me to be miserable. *(She runs off to the right with her misery and leaves Sir Peter alone with his.)*

SIR PETER: Was ever man so crossed as I am? Everything conspiring to fret me! I had not been involved in matrimony a fortnight, before her father, a hale and hearty man, died, on purpose, I believe, for the pleasure of plaguing me with the care of his daughter. *(suddenly aware of a melodious happy humming coming from the left and catching sight of his other plague, also just returned from Lady Sneerwell's)* But here comes my helpmate! She appears in great good humor. *(in the dour manner of the lonely heart)* How happy I should be if I could tease her into loving me, though but a little!

Lady Teazle comes into the room, quietly concluding her blithe melody.

LADY TEAZLE: *(in high good spirits)* Lud! Sir Peter, I hope you hav'n't been quarreling with Maria? It is not using me well to be ill-humored when I am not by.

SIR PETER: *(gently)* Ah! Lady Teazle, you might have the power to make me good-humored at all times.

LADY TEAZLE: I am sure I wish I had; for I want you to be in a charming sweet temper at this moment. Do be good-humored now, and let me have two hundred pounds, will you?

SIR PETER: *(charmed)* Two hundred pounds! What, a'n't I to be in a good humor without paying for it? But speak to me thus, and i' faith there's nothing I could refuse you. *(taking out his wallet)* You shall have it; but seal me a bond for the repayment. *(He attempts to kiss her.)*

LADY TEAZLE: *(in her most beguiling manner)* Oh no— there. *(She holds out her hand to him.)* My note of hand will do as well.

SIR PETER: *(taking her hand and kissing it with every evidence of his delight)* And you shall no longer reproach me with not giving you an independent settlement. I mean shortly to surprise you. But *(hope again triumphing over experience)* shall we live ever thus, hey?

LADY TEAZLE: If you please. *(playfully)* I'm sure I don't care how soon we leave off quarreling, provided you'll own you were tired first.

SIR PETER: *(refusing to be needled)* Well, then let our future contest be, who shall be most obliging.

LADY TEAZLE: *(affectionately taking his arm)* I assure you, Sir Peter, good nature becomes you. You look now as you did before we were married, when you used to walk with me under the elms, and tell me stories of what a gallant you were in your youth, and chuck me under the chin, you would, and ask me if I thought I could love an old fellow, who would deny me nothing—didn't you?

SIR PETER: *(close to rapture)* Yes, yes; and you were as kind and attentive—

LADY TEAZLE: *(unable to forego the pleasure of goading her foolishly doting spouse)* Ay, so I was, and would always take your part, when my acquaintance used to abuse you, and turn you into ridicule.

SIR PETER: *(hurt)* Indeed!

LADY TEAZLE: Ay, and when my cousin Sophy has called you a stiff, peevish old bachelor, and laughed at me for thinking of marrying one who might be my father, I have always defended you, and said, I didn't think you so ugly by any means, and I dared say you'd make a very good sort of a husband.

SIR PETER: *(determined to be agreeable and attributing her remarks to her innocent frankness, not to deliberate maliciousness)* And you prophesied right; and we shall now be the happiest couple—

LADY TEAZLE: And never differ again?

SIR PETER: No, never! *(with gentle reasonableness but in the mistaken tone of the elderly guardian rather than the loving husband)* Though at the same time, indeed, my dear Lady Teazle, you must watch your temper very seriously; for in all our little quarrels, my dear, if you recollect, my love, you always began first.

LADY TEAZLE: *(in a tone of reprimand)* I beg your pardon, my dear Sir Peter: indeed, you always gave the provocation.

SIR PETER: *(his voice edged with irritation)* Now see, my angel! take care; contradicting isn't the way to keep friends.

LADY TEAZLE: *(sharply)* Then don't you begin it, my love!

SIR PETER: There, now! you—*(his affection dissolving in exasperation)* you are going on. *(with a renewed attempt at gentle reasoning)* You don't perceive, my life, that you are just doing the very thing which you know always makes me angry.

LADY TEAZLE: Nay, you know if you will be angry without any reason, my dear—

SIR PETER: *(at last abandoning the honeyed tone)* There! now you want to quarrel again.

LADY TEAZLE: *(quarrelsomely denying it)* No, I am sure I don't; but if you will be so peevish—

SIR PETER: *(clumsily seeking justification)* There now! who begins first?

LADY TEAZLE: Why you, to be sure. I said nothing; but there's no bearing your temper.

SIR PETER: No, no, madam; the fault's in your own temper.

LADY TEAZLE: *(warming to the battle)* Ay, you are just what my cousin Sophy said you would be.

SIR PETER: *(sharply)* Your cousin Sophy is a forward, impertinent gipsy.

LADY TEAZLE: You are a great bear, I'm sure, to abuse my relations.

SIR PETER: Now may all the plagues of marriage be double on me, if ever I try to be friends with you any more!

LADY TEAZLE: So much the better.

SIR PETER: No, no, madam; *(grimly as though facing a withering truth)* 'tis evident you never cared a pin for me, and I was a madman to marry you—a pert, rural coquette, that had refused half the honest squires in the neighborhood.

LADY TEAZLE: *(brightly as though facing a grotesque truth)* And I am sure I was a fool to marry you—an old dangling bachelor, who was single at fifty, only because he never could meet with anyone who would have him.

SIR PETER: Ay, ay, madam; but you were pleased enough to listen to me; you never had such an offer before.

LADY TEAZLE: No! didn't I refuse Sir Tivy Terrier, who everybody said would have been a better match? for his estate is just as good as yours, *(wistfully thinking of opportunity lost)* and he has broke his neck since we have been married.

SIR PETER: *(choked with rage)* I have done with you, madam! You are an unfeeling, ungrateful—but there's an end to everything. I believe you capable of everything that is bad. Yes, madam, I now believe the reports relative to you and Charles, madam. Yes, madam, *you* and Charles are—not without grounds—

LADY TEAZLE: *(caught off guard and for the first time speaking in real anger)* Take care, Sir Peter; you had better not insinuate any such thing! I'll not be suspected without cause, I promise you.

SIR PETER: Very well, madam! very well! A separate maintenance as soon as you please. Yes, madam, or a divorce! I'll make an example of myself for the benefit of all old bachelors. Let us separate, madam.

LADY TEAZLE: *(regaining her customary aplomb)* Agreed, agreed. And now, my dear Sir Peter, we are of a mind once more, we may be the happiest couple, and never differ again, you know—ha! ha! ha! Well, you are going to be in a passion, I see, and I shall only interrupt you; *(goes off in high good humor)* so, bye—bye!

SIR PETER: *(alone)* Plagues and tortures. Can't I make her angry either? Oh, I am the most miserable fellow! But I'll not bear her presuming to keep her temper. No! she may break my heart, but she sha'n't keep her temper. *(follows her off stage to the right.)*

Scene Two

The reception room in Charles Surface's house, a handsome room singularly devoid of its usual furnishings which have been sacrificed to the creditors. Charles's servant Trip, himself a young dandy of no mean pretensions, ushers in Sir Oliver and Moses from the outer door to the left. His manner suggests that his sensibilities are somewhat pained at having to admit such riff-raff to the house. He is supercilious, in the gentleman's gentleman manner, throughout the scene.

TRIP: *(in a haughty tone of voice)* Here, Master Moses! if you'll stay a moment, I'll try whether—what's the gentleman's name?

SIR OLIVER: *(whispering)* Mr. Moses, what is my name?

MOSES: Mr. Premium.

TRIP: *(condescendingly)* Premium—very well. *(As he goes off to the right to announce them, he delicately takes a snuff-box from his pocket and applies a pinch of snuff to his nostrils as though it were a social disinfectant.)*

SIR OLIVER: To judge by the servants, one wouldn't believe the master was ruined. *(looking about the room and barely recognizing it)* But what!—sure, this was my brother's house?

MOSES: Yes, sir; Mr. Charles bought it of Mr. Joseph, with the furniture, pictures, etc., just as the old gentleman left it. Sir Peter thought it a piece of extravagance in him.

SIR OLIVER: *(confirmed in his original impression of the two brothers)* In my mind, the other's economy in selling it to him was more reprehensible by half.

Trip reappears.

TRIP: My master says you must wait, gentlemen; he has company, and can't speak with you yet.

SIR OLIVER: If he knew who it was wanted to see him, perhaps he would not send such a message?

TRIP: *(a little impatiently)* Yes, yes, sir; he knows you are here. I did not forget little Premium; no, no, no.

SIR OLIVER: Very well; and I pray, sir, what may be your name?

TRIP: Trip, sir; my name is Trip, at your service.

SIR OLIVER: Well, then, Mr. Trip, you have a pleasant sort of place here, I guess?

TRIP: *(loftily—with airy grandeur)* Why, yes; here are three or four of us pass our time agreeably enough; but then our wages are sometimes a little in arrear—and not very great either—but fifty pounds a year, and find our own bags and bouquets.[1]

SIR OLIVER: *(clearly shocked by this kind of extravagance, aside)* Bags and bouquets! halters and bastinadoes!

TRIP: *(speaking as gentleman to servitor)* And, á propos, Moses; have you been able to get me that little bill discounted?

[1] Furnish their own bag wigs and shoulder bouquets.

SIR OLIVER: *(aside)* Wants to raise money too! mercy on me! Has his distress too, I warrant, like a lord, and affects creditors and duns.

MOSES: 'Twas not to be done, indeed, Mr. Trip.

TRIP: *(with lordly disdain)* Good lack, you surprise me! My friend Brush has indorsed it, and I thought when he put his name on the back of a bill 'twas the same as cash.

MOSES: No! 'twouldn't do.

TRIP: A small sum; but twenty pounds. Hark'ee, Moses, do you think you couldn't get it me by way of annuity?

SIR OLIVER: *(aside)* An annuity! ha! ha! a footman raise money by way of annuity! Well done, luxury, egad!

MOSES: Well, but you must insure your place.

TRIP: Oh, with all my heart! I'll insure my place, and my life, too, if you please.

SIR OLIVER: *(aside)* It is more than I would your neck.

MOSES: But is there nothing you could deposit?

TRIP: Why, nothing capital of my master's wardrobe has dropped lately; but I could give you a mortgage on some of his winter clothes, with equity of redemption before November; or you shall have the reversion of the French velvet, or a post-obit on the blue and silver:[2] these, I should think, Moses, with a few pair of point ruffles, as a collateral security; *(imitating his master's best careless manner)* hey, my little fellow?

MOSES: Well, well. *(A bell sounds.)*

TRIP: Egad, I heard the bell! I believe, gentlemen, I can now introduce you. Don't forget the annuity, little Moses! *(with a wave of the hand)* This way, gentlemen. I'll insure my place, you know.

SIR OLIVER: *(following Moses on their way to another room)* If the man be a shadow of the master, this is a temple of dissipation indeed!

---

[2] A pledge of a blue and silver suit of clothes in expectation of its being passed on from Charles to Trip at some time in the future.

Scene Three

The game room in the same house. Charles Surface, two of his cronies Sir Harry Bumper and Careless, and several others are discovered sitting at a large table in the midst of a drinking party. On the table are scattered bottles, glasses, decanters, and a bowl of fruit. A side table at the right, flanked by two extra chairs, is loaded with extra glasses and bottles of wine. Charles lounges at the head of the table in a large armchair which rests on a slightly raised platform so that he is higher than his friends who sit on either side of the table. They are all expensively and fashionably dressed though their clothing shows some signs of dishevelment as they lounge in careless attitudes. Although by no means drunk, they are highly exhilarated and speak with unnecessary emphasis and volume.

CHARLES: *(in the amused manner of the moralizing rake)* 'Fore heaven, 'tis true! there's the great degeneracy of the age. Many of our acquaintance have taste, spirit, and politeness; but plague on't, they won't drink.

CARELESS: It is so indeed, Charles! they give in to all the substantial luxuries of the table, and abstain from nothing but wine and wit. Oh certainly society suffers by it intolerably; for now, instead of the social spirit of raillery that used to mantle over a glass of bright Burgundy, their conversation is become just like the Spawater they drink, which has all the pertness and flatulence of Champagne, without its spirit or flavor.

1ST GENTLEMAN: *(as though enunciating "the problem of our time")* But what are they to do who love play better than wine?

CARELESS: True! there's Sir Harry diets himself for gaming, and is now under a hazard[1] regimen.

CHARLES: Then he'll have the worst of it. What! you wouldn't train a horse for the course by keeping him from corn? For my part, egad, I am never so successful

---

[1] An early form of dice or craps. A hazard regimen would be a diet of dice.

as when I am a little merry; let me throw a bottle of Champagne, and I never lose; at least I never feel my losses, which is exactly the same thing.

2ND GENTLEMAN: Ay, that I believe.

CHARLES: *(in a mood of alcoholic earnestness)* And then, what man can pretend to be a believer in love, who is an abjurer of wine? 'Tis the test by which the lover knows his own heart. Fill a dozen bumpers to a dozen beauties, and she that floats atop is the maid that has bewitched you.

CARELESS: Now then, Charles, be honest, and give us your real favorite.

CHARLES: Why, I have withheld her only in compassion to you. If I toast her, you must give a round of her peers, which is impossible—on earth.

CARELESS: Oh! then we'll find some canonized vestals or heathen goddesses that will do, I warrant!

CHARLES: *(raising his glass)* Here then, bumpers, you rogues! bumpers! Maria! Maria! *(They all drink.)*

SIR HARRY: Maria who?

CHARLES: *(sober enough to retain some discretion)* Oh, damn the surname! 'Tis too formal to be registered in Love's calendar; but now, Sir Harry, beware, we must have beauty superlative.

CARELESS: Nay, never study,[2] Sir Harry; we'll stand to the toast, though your mistress should want an eye, and you know you have a song will excuse you.

SIR HARRY: Egad, so I have! and I'll give him the song instead of the lady. *(He sings gustily.)*

> Here's to the maiden of bashful fifteen;
>> Here's to the widow of fifty;
> Here's to the flaunting extravagant queen,
>> And here's to the housewife that's thrifty.

(All join in the chorus)
>> Let the toast pass,
>> Drink to the lass,
> I'll warrant she'll prove an excuse for the glass.

---
[2] Have no fear.

SIR HARRY:
 Here's to the charmer whose dimples we prize;
  Now to the maid who has none, sir;
 Here's to the girl with a pair of blue eyes,
  And here's to the nymph with but *one*, sir.
CHORUS:
   Let the toast pass, *etc.*
SIR HARRY:
 Here's to the maid with a bosom of snow;
  Now to her that's as brown as a berry;
 Here's to the wife with a face full of woe,
  And now to the girl that is merry.
CHORUS:
   Let the toast pass, *etc.*
SIR HARRY:
 For let 'em be clumsy, or let 'em be slim,
  Young or ancient, I care not a feather;
 So fill a pint bumper quite up to the brim,
  And let us e'en toast them together.
CHORUS:
   Let the toast pass, *etc.*

ALL: *(shouting)* Bravo! bravo! *(Amidst the applause, Trip enters from the left unobtrusively and whispers to Charles, who nods to him and rises from his place at the head of the table.)*

CHARLES: Gentlemen, you must excuse me a little. Careless, take the chair, will you?

CARELESS: *(with a sly wink at the others)* Nay, pr'ythee, Charles, what now? This is one of your peerless beauties, I suppose, has dropt in by chance?

CHARLES: *(laughing)* No, faith! To tell you the truth, 'tis a Jew and a broker, who are come by appointment.

CARELESS: *(unwilling to deprive the party of Charles or to miss any opportunity for fun)* Oh, damn it! let's have the Jew in.

1ST GENTLEMAN: *(enthusiastically)* Ay, and the broker too, by all means.

2ND GENTLEMAN: Yes, yes, the Jew and the broker.

CHARLES: *(catching the spirit of possible fun in store*

by mass baiting of the money-lenders) Egad, with all my heart! *(to Trip)* Trip, bid the gentlemen walk in. *(Trip exits as Charles turns to the group to inject a word of warning.)* Though there's one of them a stranger, I can tell you.

CARELESS: Charles, let us give them some generous Burgundy, and perhaps they'll grow conscientious.

CHARLES: Oh, hang 'em, no! wine does but draw forth a man's natural qualities, and to make them drink would only be to whet their knavery.

Trip reappears to usher in Sir Oliver Surface and Moses.

CHARLES: *(welcoming them)* So, honest Moses, walk in; walk in, pray, Mr. Premium—that's the gentleman's name, isn't it, Moses?

MOSES: *(ill at ease and rather unhappy)* Yes, sir.

CHARLES: *(expansively)* Set chairs, Trip—sit down, Mr. Premium—glasses, Trip—sit down, Moses. *(As directed, Trip pulls forward the two chairs to the table and provides glasses.)* Come, Mr. Premium, I'll give you a sentiment; here's *Success to usury!* Moses, fill the gentleman a bumper. *(The guests sit down rather uneasily as Moses fills their glasses in a rather gingerly manner.)*

MOSES: *(woodenly)* Success to usury! *(He drinks.)*

CARELESS: Right, Moses; usury is prudence and industry, and deserves to succeed.

SIR OLIVER: *(simultaneously annoyed and amused)* Then here's *All the success it deserves!* *(He drinks.)*

CARELESS: *(rising vehemently)* No, no, that won't do! Mr. Premium, you have demurred at the toast, and must drink it in a pint bumper.

1ST GENTLEMAN: *(joining the fun)* A pint bumper, at least. *(They all rise and surround Moses.)*

MOSES: *(defensively)* Oh, pray, sir, consider; Mr. Premium's a gentleman.

CARELESS: *(with enthusiasm)* And therefore loves good wine.

2ND GENTLEMAN: *(in mock anger)* Give Moses a quart glass; this is mutiny, and a high contempt for the chair.

CARELESS: *(agreeing)* Here, now for't! *(He empties a bottle into the glass.)* I'll see justice done, to the last drop of my bottle.

SIR OLIVER: *(weakly)* Nay, pray, gentlemen; I did not expect this usage.

CHARLES: *(his innate decency asserting itself)* No, hang it, Careless, you sha'n't! Mr. Premium's a stranger.

SIR OLIVER: *(aside)* Odd![3] I wish I was well out of this company.

CARELESS: Plague on 'em, then! If they won't drink, we'll not sit down with them. Come, Harry, the dice are in the next room. Charles, you'll join us when you have finished your business with the gentlemen?

CHARLES: *(really pleased by their departure)* I will! I will! *(They begin to file out to the right.)* Careless!

CARELESS: *(stopping and turning)* Well!

CHARLES: Perhaps I may want you.

CARELESS: *(understanding)* Oh, you know I am always ready: word, note, or bond, 'tis all the same to me. *(He follows the group to the next room.)*

MOSES: *(relieved and getting down to business)* Sir, this is Mr. Premium, a gentleman of the strictest honor and secrecy; and always performs what he undertakes. Mr. Premium, this is—

CHARLES: *(interrupting the standardized advertising speech of Moses with impatience)* Pshaw! have done. *(to Sir Oliver)* Sir, my friend Moses is a very honest fellow, but a little slow at expression: he'll be an hour giving us our titles. Mr. Premium, the plain state of the matter is this: I am an extravagant young fellow who wants to borrow money; you I take to be a prudent old fellow, who has got money to lend. I am blockhead enough to give fifty percent sooner than not to have it; and you, I presume, are rogue enough to take a hundred if you can get it. Now, sir, you see we are acquainted at once, and may proceed without further ceremony.

SIR OLIVER: *(pleased)* Exceeding frank, upon my word. I see, sir, you are not a man of many compliments.

---

[3] Euphemism for *God!*

CHARLES: Oh, no, sir! plain dealing in business I always think best.

SIR OLIVER: Sir, I like you the better for it. However, you are mistaken in one thing; I have no money to lend, but I believe I could procure some of a friend; but then he's an unconscionable dog, isn't he, Moses?

MOSES: But you can't help that.

SIR OLIVER: *(an apt pupil)* And must sell stock to accommodate you—mustn't he, Moses?

MOSES: Yes, indeed! You know I always speak the truth, and scorn to tell a lie!

CHARLES: *(again showing irritation at his verboseness)* People that speak truth generally do; but these are trifles, Mr. Premium. What! I know money isn't to be bought without paying for 't!

SIR OLIVER: Well, but what security could you give? You have no land, I suppose?

CHARLES: Not a molehill, nor a twig, but what's in the bough-pots[4] out of the window!

SIR OLIVER: Nor any stock, I presume?

CHARLES: Nothing but live stock, and that's only a few pointers and ponies. But pray, Mr. Premium, are you acquainted at all with any of my connections?

SIR OLIVER: *(amused by the ironic question)* Why, to say truth, I am.

CHARLES: Then you must know that I have a dev'lish rich uncle in the East Indies, Sir Oliver Surface, from whom I have the greatest expectations.

SIR OLIVER: *(drily)* That you have a wealthy uncle I have heard; but how your expectations will turn out is more, I believe, than you can tell.

CHARLES: *(with easy confidence)* Oh, no! there can be no doubt. They tell me I'm a prodigious favorite, and that he talks of leaving me everything.

SIR OLIVER: Indeed! this is the first I've heard of it.

CHARLES: Yes, yes, 'tis just so. Moses knows 'tis true; don't you, Moses?

---

[4] Flower-pots.

MOSES: Oh, yes! I'll swear to 't.

SIR OLIVER: *(aside)* Egad, they'll persuade me presently I'm at Bengal.

CHARLES: Now, I propose, Mr. Premium, if it's agreeable to you, a post-obit on Sir Oliver's life; though at the same time the old fellow has been so liberal to me, that I give you my word, I should be very sorry to hear that anything had happened to him.

SIR OLIVER: Not more than I should, I assure you. But the bond you mention happens to be just the worst security you could offer me, for I might live to a hundred, and never see the principal.

CHARLES: *(sincerely)* Oh, yes, you would; the moment Sir Oliver dies, you know, you would come on me for the money.

SIR OLIVER: *(hoping to educe from Charles some further statement of his feeling for his uncle)* Then I believe I should be the most unwelcome dun you ever had in your life.

CHARLES: *(assuming that Mr. Premium's only concern is for his money)* What! I suppose you're afraid that Sir Oliver is too good a life?

SIR OLIVER: No, indeed, I am not; though I have heard he is as hale and healthy as any man of his years in Christendom.

CHARLES: There again now you are misinformed. No, no, the climate has hurt him considerably, poor uncle Oliver! Yes, yes, he breaks apace, I'm told, and is so much altered lately, that his nearest relations don't know him.

SIR OLIVER: *(unable to contain himself)* No! ha! ha! ha! so much altered lately, that his nearest relations don't know him! ha! ha! ha! *(gasping for breath)* egad—ha! ha! ha!

CHARLES: *(attributing this unseemly mirth to rapacity)* Ha! ha! you're glad to hear that, little Premium?

SIR OLIVER: *(attempting to recover his equilibrium)* No, no, I'm not.

CHARLES: *(scornfully)* Yes, yes, you are—ha! ha! ha! You know that mends your chance.

SIR OLIVER: But I'm told Sir Oliver is coming over. Nay, some say he is actually arrived.

CHARLES: *(with a grandiose wave of the hand)* Pshaw! Sure I must know better than you whether he's come or not. No, no; rely on't, he's at this moment at Calcutta. Isn't he, Moses?

MOSES: *(blinking rapidly and looking smug)* Oh, yes, certainly.

SIR OLIVER: Very true, as you say, you must know better than I, though I have it from pretty good authority. Haven't I, Moses?

MOSES: *(with the same bland manner)* Yes, most undoubted!

SIR OLIVER: *(his voice assuming a more practical tone)* But, sir, as I understand you want a few hundreds immediately, is there nothing you could dispose of?

CHARLES: How do you mean?

SIR OLIVER: For instance, now, I have heard that your father left behind a great quantity of massive old plate?

CHARLES: Oh, Lud! that's gone long ago. Moses can tell you how better than I can.

SIR OLIVER: *(aside)* Good lack! all the family race-cups and corporation-bowls! *(to Charles)* —Then it was also supposed that his library was one of the most valuable and compact—

CHARLES: Yes, yes, so it was—vastly too much so for a private gentleman. *(in a tone of condescending benevolence)* For my part, I was always of a communicative disposition, so I thought it a shame to keep so much knowledge to myself.

SIR OLIVER: *(aside, startled by such easy charity)* Mercy upon me! Learning that had run in the family like an heirloom! *(to Charles)* —Pray, what are become of the books?

CHARLES: You must enquire of the auctioneer, Master Premium, for I don't believe even Moses can direct you.

MOSES: *(factually)* I know nothing of books.

SIR OLIVER: So, so, nothing of the family property left, I suppose?

CHARLES: *(with no apparent sense of shame or concern)* Not much, indeed; unless you have a mind to the family pictures. I have got a room full of ancestors above, and if you have a taste for paintings, egad, you shall have 'em a bargain.

SIR OLIVER: *(more shocked than ever)* Hey! what the devil! sure, you wouldn't sell your forefathers, would you?

CHARLES: *(cheerfully and greatly amused)* Every man of them to the best bidder.

SIR OLIVER: *(unable to believe what he hears)* What! your great uncles and aunts?

CHARLES: Ay, and my great grandfathers and grand-mothers too.

SIR OLIVER: *(aside)* Now I give him up. *(close to betraying himself, to Charles)* What the plague, have you no bowels for your own kindred? Odd's life, do you take me for Shylock in the play, that you would raise money of me on your own flesh and blood?

CHARLES: *(soothingly)* Nay, my little broker, don't be angry: what need *you* care if you have your money's worth?

SIR OLIVER: *(heavily and sternly)* Well, I'll be the purchaser: I think I can dispose of the family canvas— *(aside as Careless enters)* Oh, I'll never forgive him this! never!

CARELESS: *(impatient)* Come, Charles, what keeps you?

CHARLES: I can't come yet: i'faith we are going to have a sale above stairs. Here's little Premium will buy all my ancestors.

CARELESS: *(annoyed)* Oh, burn your ancestors!

CHARLES: *(amused)* No, he may do that afterwards, if he pleases. *(Careless moves as if to return to the party.)* Stay, Careless, we want you; egad, you shall be our auctioneer; so come along with us.

CARELESS: *(agreeably)* Oh, have with you, if that's

the case. I can handle a hammer as well as a dice-box!

SIR OLIVER: *(aside)* Oh, the profligates!

CHARLES: Come, Moses, you shall be appraiser, if we want one. *(unable to comprehend Mr. Premium's strange attitude)* Gad's life, little Premium, you don't seem to like the business?

SIR OLIVER: *(recovering sufficiently to resume his masquerade)* Oh, yes, I do, vastly. *(forcing a laugh)* Ha! ha! ha! yes, yes, I think it a rare joke to sell one's family by auction—ha! ha!— *(aside, with a groan)* Oh, the prodigal!

CHARLES: *(merrily leading the way to the door at the left)* To be sure, when a man wants money, where the plague should he get assistance if he can't make free with his own relations? *(He gives Sir Oliver a hearty clap on the shoulder as they go out.)*

ACT FOUR

Scene One

The picture room or private art gallery of the Surface home. The walls are softly colored to give prominence to the striking series of large portraits which all but completely cover the rear wall. A painting of Sir Oliver himself is prominently displayed in the center. A heavy cabinet in the right-hand corner, standing somewhat above waist level, contains ancestral documents. Beside it is a large armchair, too worn to have been worth selling. The only other piece of furniture in the room is a decrepit settee, placed beneath the portrait of Sir Oliver. As the scene begins, Charles Surface and Careless are escorting the money-lenders into the room from the left.

CHARLES: *(leading the way)* Walk in, gentlemen; pray walk in. Here they are, the family of the Surfaces, up to the Conquest.

SIR OLIVER: *(sourly)* And, in my opinion, a goodly collection.

CHARLES: *(in an exaggerated burlesque of the manner of a connoisseur of art but with genuinely magnificent unconcern about the subjects themselves)* Ay, ay; these are done in the true spirit of portrait painting; no *volontière grace*[1] or expression. Not like the works of your modern Raphaels, who give you the strongest resemblance, yet contrive to make your portrait independent of you; so that you may sink the original and not hurt the picture. No, no; the merit of these is the inveterate likeness *(with a sweeping gesture that terminates by pointing*

---

[1] Added attractiveness.

directly at Sir Oliver's portrait) —all stiff and awkward as the originals, and like nothing in human nature besides.

SIR OLIVER: *(feelingly)* Ah! we shall never see such figures of men again.

CHARLES: I hope not. Well, you see, Master Premium, what a domestic character I am. *(with mock gravity)* Here I sit of an evening surrounded by my family. *(turning vivaciously to Careless)* But come, get to your pulpit, Mr. Auctioneer; here's an old gouty chair of my grandfather's will answer the purpose.

CARELESS: *(pushing the chair in the corner behind the cabinet)* Ay, ay, this will do. But, Charles, I hav'n't a hammer; and what's an auctioneer without his hammer?

CHARLES: Egad, that's true. *(opens the cabinet and reaches inside)* What parchment have we here? *(pulls out a scroll wound around a mahogany baton)* Oh, our genealogy in full. Here, Careless, you shall have no common bit of mahogany; here's the family tree for you, you rogue; this shall be your hammer, and now you may knock down my ancestors with their own pedigree.

SIR OLIVER: *(aside)* What an unnatural rogue! an *ex post facto*[2] parricide!

CARELESS: Yes, yes, here's a list of your generation indeed; faith, Charles, this is the most convenient thing you could have found for the business, for 'twill serve not only as a hammer, but a catalogue into the bargain. Come, begin—A-going, a-going, a-going!

CHARLES: *(applauding his auctioneering technique)* Bravo, Careless! *(pointing dramatically to the first portrait in the series)* Well, here's my great uncle, Sir Richard Raveline, a marvelous good general in his day, I assure you. He served in all the Duke of Marlborough's wars, and got that cut over his eye at the battle of Malplaquet. What say you, Mr. Premium? Look at him; there's a hero, not cut out of his feathers, as your modern clipp'd captains are, but enveloped in wig and regi-

---

[2] After the event is concluded.

mentals, as a general should be. What do you bid?

MOSES: *(after a whispered word from Sir Oliver)* Mr. Premium would have *you* speak.

CHARLES: *(lightly abandoning the military)* Why, then, he shall have him for ten pounds, and I'm sure that's not dear for a staff-officer.

SIR OLIVER: *(aside)* Heaven deliver me! his famous uncle Richard for ten pounds! *(to Charles)* —Well, sir, I take him at that.

CHARLES: *(in a professional manner)* Careless, knock down my uncle Richard. *(moving to the next painting)* Here, now is a maiden sister of his, my great-aunt Deborah, done by Kneller, thought to be in his best manner, and a very formidable likeness. There she is, you see, a shepherdess feeding her flock. You shall have her for five pounds ten; the sheep are worth the money.

SIR OLIVER: *(aside)* Ah! poor Deborah! a woman who set such a value on herself! *(to Charles)* Five pounds ten; she's mine.

CHARLES: *(with ribald lack of gallantry)* Knock down my aunt Deborah! Here, now, are two that were a sort of cousins of theirs. You see, Moses, these pictures were done sometime ago, when beaux wore wigs, and the ladies their own hair.

SIR OLIVER: Yes, truly, headdresses appear to have been a little lower in those days.

CHARLES: Well, take that couple for the same.

MOSES: 'Tis a good bargain.

CHARLES: Careless! This, now, is a grandfather of my mother, a learned judge, well known on the Western Circuit. What do you rate him at, Moses?

MOSES: Four guineas.

CHARLES: *(outraged)* Four guineas! Gad's life, you don't bid me the price of his wig. Mr. Premium, you have more respect for the woolsack;[3] do let us knock his lordship down at fifteen .

SIR OLIVER: *(in quiet, cynical weariness.)* By all means.

---

[3] Wool-stuffed seats for the use of judges.

CARELESS: Gone!

CHARLES: And there are two brothers of his, William and Walter Blunt, Esquires, both members of Parliament, and noted speakers, and what's very extraordinary, I believe, this is the first time they were ever bought or sold.

SIR OLIVER: *(taking heart as he appreciates the tribute to the family honor)* That is very extraordinary, indeed! I'll take them at your own price, for the honor of Parliament.

CARELESS: Well said, little Premium! I'l knock them down at forty.

CHARLES: *(moving rapidly over the portrait of Sir Oliver to the one beyond)* Here's a jolly fellow; I don't know what relation, but he was mayor of Manchester. Take him at eight pounds.

SIR OLIVER: *(so struck by Charles's previous remark about the Blunts that he is actually beginning to enjoy the nonsense)* No, no; six will do for the mayor.

CHARLES: Come, make it guineas, and I'll throw you the two aldermen there into the bargain.

SIR OLIVER: They're mine.

CHARLES: Careless, knock down the mayor and aldermen. But plague on't, we shall be all day retailing in this manner. Do let us deal wholesale! what say you, little Premium? Give us three hundred pounds for the rest of the family in a lump.

CARELESS: *(anxious to get back to the party)* Ay, ay, that will be the best way.

SIR OLIVER: Well, well, anything to accommodate you —they are mine. *(with an edge of curiosity in his manner)* But there is one portrait which you have always passed over.

CARELESS: *(who has noted the omission too)* What, that ill-looking little fellow over the settee?

SIR OLIVER: *(warming to the issue)* Yes, sir, I mean that; though I don't think him so ill-looking a little fellow, by any means.

CHARLES: What, that? Oh! that's my uncle Oliver; 'twas done before he went to India.

CARELESS: *(surprised)* Your uncle Oliver! Gad, then, you'll never be friends, Charles. That, now, to me, is as stern a looking rogue as ever I saw—an unforgiving eye, and a damned disinheriting countenance! an inveterate knave, depend on't. Don't you think so, little Premium? *(slapping him on the shoulder)*

SIR OLIVER: *(with some heat)* Upon my soul, sir, I do not. I think it is as honest a looking face as any in the room, dead or alive. *(turning to Charles)* But I suppose uncle Oliver goes with the rest of the lumber?

CHARLES: *(vehemently and with a sudden change of mood)* No, hang it! I'll not part with poor Noll. *(dusting off the picture with his handkerchief)* The old fellow has been very good to me, and egad, I'll keep his picture while I've a room to put it in.

SIR OLIVER: *(aside—bubbling suddenly like an uncorked champagne bottle)* The rogue's my nephew after all! *(turning to Charles with intense earnestness)* —But, sir, I have somehow taken a fancy to that picture.

CHARLES: *(with an air of finality)* I'm sorry for't, for you certainly will not have it. Oons, haven't you got enough of them?

SIR OLIVER: *(aside—his eyes dancing with elation)* I forgive him everything! *(pressingly, to Charles)* But, sir, when I take a whim in my head I don't value money. I'll give you as much for that as for all the rest.

CHARLES: *(angrily and with aloof dignity)* Don't tease me, master broker. I tell you I'll not part with it, and there's an end of it.

SIR OLIVER: *(aside—totally converted)* How like his father the dog is! *(to Charles)* Well, well, I have done. *(aside as he pulls a wallet from his pocket and draws out a draft)* I did not perceive it before, but I think I never saw such a striking resemblance. *(handing Charles the paper)* Here is a draft for your sum.

CHARLES: *(scrutinizing the draft and noting with pop-*

ping eyes that the amount is considerably more than the total brought by the auction) Why, 'tis for eight hundred pounds.

SIR OLIVER: *(in a final test)* You will not let Sir Oliver go?

CHARLES: *(irritated at his persistence)* Zounds! no! I tell you once more.

SIR OLIVER: Then never mind the difference, we'll balance that another time. *(lifted suddenly on a wave of impulse)* But give me your hand on the bargain; you are an honest fellow, Charles. *(remembering that this kind of behavior does not suit his role)* I beg pardon, sir, for being so free. Come, Moses.

CHARLES: Egad, this is a whimsical old fellow! But hark'ee, Premium, you'll prepare lodgings for these gentlemen? *(pointing to the portraits)*

SIR OLIVER: Yes, yes, I'll send for them in a day or two.

CHARLES: But, hold; do now send a genteel conveyance for them, for, I assure you, they were most of them used to ride in their own carriages.

SIR OLIVER: I will, I will; *(with vast delight)* for all but Oliver.

CHARLES: Ay, all but the little nabob.

SIR OLIVER: *(making doubly sure of his ground)* You're fixed on that?

CHARLES: Peremptorily

SIR OLIVER: *(aside)* A dear extravagant rogue! *(to Charles and Careless)* Good day! Come, Moses. *(to himself)* Let me hear now who dares call him profligate!

Sir Oliver and Moses go off to the left. When safely out of earshot, Charles and Careless burst into laughter.

CARELESS: *(bemused)* Why, this is the oddest genius of the sort I ever saw!

CHARLES: Egad! he's the prince of brokers, I think. I wonder how Moses got acquainted with so honest a fellow. *(looking with pleasure toward the wings through which they have just disappeared)* Ha! here's Rowley.

Do, Careless, say I'll join the company in a few moments.

CARELESS: I will; *(fearful of being ruined by morality)* but don't let that old blockhead persuade you to squander any of that money on old musty debts, or any such nonsense; for tradesmen, Charles, are the most exorbitant fellows.

CHARLES: *(anxious to suppress vice)* Very true, and paying them is only encouraging them.

CARELESS: *(loftily)* Nothing else.

CHARLES: *(to Careless as he leaves)* Ay, ay, never fear. *(musing aloud)* So! this was an odd old fellow, indeed. Let me see; two-thirds of this is mine by right, five hundred and thirty odd pounds. 'Fore heaven! I find one's ancestors are more valuable relations than I took them for! *(bowing deeply and ceremoniously to the portraits)* Ladies and gentlemen, your most obedient and very grateful servant. *(straightens to perceive Rowley's entrance)* Ha! old Rowley! egad, you are just come in time to take leave of your old acquaintance.

ROWLEY: Yes, I heard they were a-going. But I wonder you can have such spirits under so many distresses.

CHARLES: Why, there's the point! my distresses are so many, that I can't afford to part with my spirits; but I shall be rich and splenetic, all in good time. However, I suppose you are surprised that I am not more sorrowful at parting with so many near relations. To be sure 'tis very affecting; but you see they never move a muscle, so why should I?

ROWLEY: *(indulgently)* There's no making you serious a moment.

CHARLES: *(soberly)* Yes, faith, I am so now. *(holding out the draft)* Here, my honest Rowley, here, get me this changed directly, and take a hundred pounds of it immediately to old Stanley.

ROWLEY: *(astonished)* A hundred pounds! Consider only—

CHARLES: *(interrupting with annoyance)* Gad's life,

don't talk about it. Poor Stanley's wants are pressing, and if you don't make haste, we shall have someone call that has a better right to the money.

ROWLEY: Ah! there's the point! I never will cease dunning you with the old proverb—

CHARLES: *(impatiently)* "Be just before you're generous." Why, so I would if I could; but Justice is an old, lame, hobbling beldame, and I can't get her to keep pace with Generosity for the soul of me.

ROWLEY: *(pleadingly)* Yet, Charles, believe me, one hour's reflection—

CHARLES: *(dismissing him abruptly)* Ay, ay, it's all very true; but, hark'ee, Rowley, while I have, by heaven, I'll give! So damn your economy!! *(Rowley bows sorrowfully and turns to go. Charles turns to the opposite door to join his company.)* And now for hazard![4] *(He goes off.)*

Scene Two

The downstairs parlor of the same house, similarly stripped of all valuable furnishings. Sir Oliver Surface and Moses pause here for discussion after leaving the picture room. As they enter from the right Sir Oliver is still elated over his nephew's behavior in spite of the sensible demurrers of Moses.

MOSES: Well, sir, I think, as Sir Peter said, you have seen Mr. Charles in high glory; 'tis great pity he's so extravagant.

SIR OLIVER: *(not to be distracted from his discovery of Charles's loyalty to him)* True, but he would not sell my picture.

MOSES: And loves wine and women so much.

SIR OLIVER: But he would not sell my picture.

MOSES: And games so deep.

SIR OLIVER: But he would not sell my picture. Oh, here's Rowley.

---

[4] Dice.

Rowley enters immediately after leaving Charles.

ROWLEY: So, Sir Oliver, I find you have made a purchase—

SIR OLIVER: Yes, yes; our young rake has parted with his ancestors like old tapestry.

ROWLEY: And here has he commissioned me to re-deliver you part of the purchase money. I mean, though, in your necessitous character of old Stanley.

MOSES: *(deploringly)* Ah! there is the pity of it all; he is so damned charitable.

ROWLEY: *(agreeing)* And I left a hosier and two tailors in the hall, who, I'm sure, won't be paid, and this hundred would satisfy them.

SIR OLIVER: *(unaffected by these considerations)* Well, well, I'll pay his debts, and his benevolence, too. But now I am no more a broker, and you shall introduce me to the elder brother as old Stanley.

ROWLEY: Not yet awhile; Sir Peter, I know, means to call there about this time.

Trip enters with a verbal apology which is not borne out by his manner.

TRIP: Oh, gentlemen, I beg pardon for not showing you out; *(waving a hand mechanically in the direction of the door at the left)* this way. *(to Moses)* Moses, a word. *(He directs Moses to the opposite door and escorts him to another room.)*

SIR OLIVER: *(alone with Rowley)* There's a fellow for you! Would you believe it, that puppy intercepted the Jew on our coming, and wanted to raise money before he got to his master.

ROWLEY: Indeed!

SIR OLIVER: Yes, they are now planning an annuity business. Ah, Master Rowley, in my days servants were content with the follies of their masters, when they were worn a little threadbare; but now, they have their vices, like their birthday clothes,[1] with the gloss on.

They go out.

---

[1] Lavish costumes worn in honor of the king's birthday.

Scene Three

The library in Joseph Surface's house. It is a large room, lined with bookshelves at the back except for a large window toward the left. Although not as intrinsically rich as the rooms in the original Surface home owned by Charles, it is completely and comfortably furnished with chairs. A casual table at the right balances an ornamental screen decorated with maps at the left. On one side of the front of the stage the proscenium door at the right opens into a large storage closet. Joseph's servant enters from the left with some letters which he places on the table. He then occupies himself with adjusting the furniture as Joseph enters from the right, goes to the table, and picks up and examines the letters without opening them.

JOSEPH: *(looking up at the servant with a slight frown)* No letter from Lady Teazle?

SERVANT: No, sir.

JOSEPH: *(troubled)* I am surprised she has not sent, if she is prevented from coming. Sir Peter certainly does not suspect me. Yet I wish I may not lose the heiress, through the scrape I have drawn myself into with the wife. However, Charles' imprudence and bad character are great points in my favor. *(The heavy sound of a brass door-knocker is heard.)*

SERVANT: Sir, I believe that must be Lady Teazle.

JOSEPH: *(nervously)* Hold! See whether it is or not before you go to the door: I have a particular message for you, if it should be my brother.

SERVANT: *(looking out the window)* 'Tis her ladyship, sir; she always leaves her chair at the milliner's in the next street. *(He makes as if to leave.)*

JOSEPH: *(on edge)* Stay, stay; draw that screen before the window. *(The servant obeys.)* That will do. My opposite neighbor is a maiden lady of so anxious a temper. *(signalling the servant to admit the visitor)* I have a difficult hand to play in this affair. *(as the servant disappears left, through the wings)* Lady Teazle has lately suspected my views on Maria; but she must by no means be let into that secret—at least, till I have her more in my power.

Lady Teazle enters in her usual infectious high spirits, all but ignoring the servant who ushers her in.

LADY TEAZLE: What, sentiment in soliloquy now? Have you been very impatient? Oh, Lud! don't pretend to look grave. I vow I couldn't come before.

JOSEPH: *(regaining his self-possession)* Oh, madam, punctuality is a species of constancy, a very unfashionable quality in a lady. *(The servant discreetly places chairs and vanishes.)*

LADY TEAZLE: *(pouting as she sits down)* Upon my word you ought to pity me. Do you know, Sir Peter is grown so ill-natured of late, and so jealous of Charles too! *(brightly but pointedly)* That's the best of the story, isn't it?

JOSEPH: *(aside)* I am glad my scandalous friends keep that up.

LADY TEAZLE: *(continuing to probe his real intentions)* I am sure I wish he would let Maria marry him, and then perhaps he would be convinced. *(tilting her head archly as she looks at him obliquely)* Don't you, Mr. Surface?

JOSEPH: *(aside)* Indeed I do not. *(reassuringly to Lady Teazle as he sits cozily beside her)* Oh, certainly I do! for then my dear Lady Teazle would also be convinced how wrong her suspicions were of my having any design on the silly girl.

LADY TEAZLE: *(soothed)* Well, well, I'm inclined to believe you. *(pouting again)* But isn't it provoking, to have the most ill-natured things said of one? And there's my friend, Lady Sneerwell, has circulated I don't know how many scandalous tales of me, and all without any foundation too! That's what vexes me.

JOSEPH: *(taking advantage of her fundamental innocence)* Ay, madam, to be sure, that is the provoking circumstance—without foundation. Yes, yes, there's the mortification, indeed; for when a scandalous story is believed against one, there certainly is no comfort like the consciousness of having deserved it.

LADY TEAZLE: *(unconscious of the intent of his innuendo)* No, to be sure, then I'd forgive their malice; but to attack me, who am really so innocent, and who never say an ill-natured thing of anybody—*(qualifying such an obvious misstatement)* that is, of any friend; and then Sir Peter too, to have him so peevish, and so suspicious, when I know the integrity of my own heart! *(working herself up to a high pitch of righteous indignation)* Indeed 'tis monstrous!

JOSEPH: *(earnestly)* But, my dear Lady Teazle, 'tis your own fault if you suffer it. When a husband entertains a groundless suspicion of his wife, and withdraws his confidence from her, the original compact is broken, and she owes it to the honor of her sex to outwit him.

LADY TEAZLE: *(beginning to understand, with a puzzled frown)* Indeed! So that if he suspects me without cause, it follows that the best way of curing his jealousy is to give him reason for't?

JOSEPH: *(with an easy air of authoritative confidence)* Undoubtedly; for your husband should never be deceived in you; and in that case it becomes you to be frail in compliment to his discernment.

LADY TEAZLE: *(uncertainly as she ponders this paradox)* To be sure, what you say is very reasonable, and when the consciousness of my innocence—

JOSEPH: *(with an air of deep solicitude and lofty morality)* Ah! my dear madam, there is the great mistake: 'tis this very conscious innocence that is of the greatest prejudice to you. What is it makes you negligent of forms, and careless of the world's opinion? Why, the consciousness of your own innocence. What makes you impatient of Sir Peter's temper, and outrageous at his suspicions? Why, the consciousness of your own innocence.

LADY TEAZLE: *(unable to refute this unassailable logic, but in a tone of something less than complete conviction)* 'Tis very true!

JOSEPH: *(with wheedling endearment)* Now, my dear Lady Teazle, if you would but once make a trifling *faux pas,* you can't conceive how cautious you would grow, and how ready to humor and agree with your husband.

LADY TEAZLE: *(really confused at this policy of domestic harmony based on infidelity)* Do you think so?

JOSEPH: *(glibly)* Oh! I'm sure on't; and then you would find all scandal would cease at once; for, in short, your character at present is like a person in a plethora, absolutely dying from too much health.

LADY TEAZLE: *(in the manner of a schoolchild finally comprehending a new principle)* So, so; then I perceive your prescription is that I must sin in my own defense, and part with my virtue to secure my reputation?

JOSEPH: *(the schoolmaster pleased at the precocity of his pupil)* Exactly so, upon my credit, ma'am.

LADY TEAZLE: *(frankly)* Well, certainly, this is the oddest doctrine and the newest receipt for avoiding calumny!

JOSEPH: *(sententiously as he familiarly attempts to take her hand)* An infallible one, believe me. Prudence, like experience, must be paid for.

LADY TEAZLE: *(wavering and drawing back)* Why, if my understanding were once convinced—

JOSEPH: *(protesting as his hand rests momentarily lightly on her knee)* Oh, certainly, madam, your understanding should be convinced. *(raising his hand as though in blessing and slightly elevating his eyes)* Yes, yes; heaven forbid I should persuade you to do anything you thought wrong. *(in a tone of unctuous intimacy)* No, no, I have too much honor to desire it.

LADY TEAZLE: *(with sudden perspicacity while rising with great dignity)* Don't you think we may as well leave *honor* out of the question?

JOSEPH: *(affecting delicate surprise as he stands up)* Ah! the ill effects of your country education, I see, still remain with you.

LADY TEAZLE: *(irritably but with still a trace of uncertainty)* I doubt they do indeed; and I will fairly own to you, that if I could be persuaded to do wrong, it would be by Sir Peter's ill-usage sooner than your *honorable logic,* after all.

JOSEPH: *(reaching out his hand to her)* Then, by this hand, which he is unworthy of—*(He takes her hand in his and is about to kneel to her just as the servant enters.)* 'Sdeath, you blockhead! What do you want?

SERVANT: I beg your pardon, sir, but I thought you would not choose Sir Peter to come up without announcing him.

JOSEPH: *(jumping up)* Sir Peter! Oons—the devil!

LADY TEAZLE: Sir Peter! Oh, Lud, I'm ruined! I'm ruined!

SERVANT: *(defensively)* Sir, 'twasn't I let him in.

LADY TEAZLE: Oh, I'm quite undone! What will become of me? *(accusingly to Joseph)* Now, Mr. Logic. *(darts a hurried look to the door and then a hurried glance around for escape or concealment)* Oh, he's on the stairs. *(running to the screen)* I'll get behind here; and if ever I'm so imprudent again—*(She subsides behind the screen.)*

JOSEPH: *(sharply to the servant)* Give me that book. *(He snatches the book from the servant's hands and sits down behind it, simulating an attitude of elaborately cool preoccupation, as the servant pretends to be tidying up.)*

Sir Peter enters blandly and perceives Joseph at his reading.

SIR PETER: Ay, ever improving himself. Mr. Surface! *(no response)* Mr. Surface!

JOSEPH: *(with a start and laughing, as it were, at his own languid abstraction)* Oh! my dear Sir Peter, I beg your pardon. *(Yawning and putting the book aside)* I have been dozing over a stupid book. Well, I am much obliged to you for this call. You haven't been here, I believe, since I fitted up this room. Books, you know, are the only things in which I am a coxcomb.

SIR PETER: *(surveying the room)* 'Tis very neat indeed. Well, well, that's proper; and you can make even your screen a source of knowledge—hung, I perceive, with maps. *(advancing toward the screen as if to examine it more closely)*

JOSEPH: *(with forced casualness as he slips between Sir Peter and the screen and waves him toward a chair)* Oh, yes, I find great use in that screen.

SIR PETER: I dare say you must, certainly, when you want to find anything in a hurry.

JOSEPH: *(aside)* Ay, to hide anything in a hurry, either.

SIR PETER: *(glancing toward the servant)* Well, I have a little private business—

JOSEPH: *(to the servant)* You need not stay.

SERVANT: No, sir. *(He bows out.)*

JOSEPH: *(pulling forward a chair with its back to the screen)* Here's a chair, Sir Peter. I beg— *(motioning him to be seated).*

SIR PETER: *(sitting down)* Well, now we are alone, there is a subject, my dear friend, on which I wish to unburden my mind to you—a point of the greatest moment to my peace; in short, my dear friend, Lady Teazle's conduct of late has made me extremely unhappy. *(Lady Teazle's head appears from behind the screen to vanish again suddenly at a sharp glance from Joseph who remains standing as if to command the situation.)*

JOSEPH: Indeed! I am very sorry to hear of it.

SIR PETER: Ay, 'tis too plain she has not the least regard for me; but, what's worse, I have pretty good authority to suppose she has formed an attachment to another.

JOSEPH: Indeed! you astonish me!

SIR PETER: Yes; and between ourselves, I think I've discovered the person. *(The head appears and disappears again in alarmed abruptness.)*

JOSEPH: How! You alarm me exceedingly.

SIR PETER: Ay, my dear friend, I knew you would sympathize with me!

JOSEPH: *(tongue in cheek as he glances nervously toward the screen)* Yes, believe me, Sir Peter, such a discovery would hurt me just as much as it would you.

SIR PETER: I am convinced of it. Ah! it is a happiness to have a friend whom we can trust even with one's family secrets. But have you no guess who I mean?

JOSEPH: *(with monumental innocence)* I haven't the most distant idea. It can't be Sir Benjamin Backbite!

SIR PETER: Oh, no! What say you to Charles?

JOSEPH: *(conveying the impression of great shock)* My brother! impossible!

SIR PETER: Oh! my dear friend, the goodness of your own heart misleads you. You judge of others by yourself.

JOSEPH: *(piously)* Certainly, Sir Peter, the heart that is conscious of its own integrity is ever slow to credit another's treachery.

SIR PETER: *(with obtuse simplicity)* True, but your brother has no sentiment; you never hear him talk so.

JOSEPH: Yet I can't but think Lady Teazle herself has too much principle.

SIR PETER: *(more brightly but unaware of his target)* Ay; but what is principle against the flattery of a handsome, lively young fellow.

JOSEPH: *(gravely)* That's very true.

SIR PETER: And there's, you know, the difference of our ages makes it very improbable that she should have any great affection for me; and if she were to be frail, and I were to make it public, why the town would only laugh at me, the foolish old bachelor who had married a girl.

JOSEPH: *(forced to agree with a bitter truth)* That's true, to be sure; they would laugh.

SIR PETER: *(contemplating the Scandal Club with anguish)* Laugh—ay, and make ballads, and paragraphs, and the devil knows what of me.

JOSEPH: *(thoughtfully and conclusively)* No, you must never make it public.

SIR PETER: But then again—that the nephew of my old friend, Sir Oliver, should be the person to attempt such a wrong, hurts me more nearly.

JOSEPH: *(sorrowfully but with some embarrassment*

as his eye again meets that of Lady Teazle whose head again quickly appears and withdraws) Ay, there's the point. When ingratitude barbs the dart of injury, the wound has double danger in it.

SIR PETER: *(his sense of being wronged mounting with this display of sympathy)* Ay, I that was, in a manner, left his guardian; in whose home he had been so often entertained; who never in my life denied him *(catching a trace of skepticism in Joseph's eye)* —my advice.

JOSEPH: *(vigorously and with superbly bold indifference to the present situation)* Oh, 'tis not to be credited. There may be a man capable of such baseness, to be sure; but for my part, till you can give me positive proofs, I cannot but doubt it. However, if it should be proved on him, he is no longer a brother of mine. I disclaim kindred with him; for the man who can break the laws of hospitality, and tempt the wife of his friend, deserves to be branded as the pest of society.

SIR PETER: *(with admiration)* What a difference there is between you! What noble sentiments!

JOSEPH: *(remembering the presence of his other guest)* Yet I cannot suspect Lady Teazle's honor.

SIR PETER: I am sure I wish to think well of her, and to remove all ground of quarrel between us. She has lately reproached me more than once with having made no settlement on her; and, in our last quarrel, she almost hinted that she should not break her heart if I was dead. Now, as we seem to differ in our ideas of expense, I have resolved she shall have her own way, and be her own mistress in that respect for the future; and if I were to die, she will find I have not been inattentive to her interest while living. Here, my friend, *(extracting legal papers from his coat pocket)* are the drafts of two deeds, which I wish to have your opinion on. *(extending the papers to Joseph)* By one, she will enjoy eight hundred a year independent while I live; and, by the other, the bulk of my fortune at my death. *(draws out his handkerchief and touches it to his eyes)*

JOSEPH: *(glancing at the deeds)* This, conduct, Sir

Peter, is indeed truly generous. *(aside)* I wish it may not corrupt my pupil.

SIR PETER: Yes, I am determined she shall have no cause to complain, though I would not have her acquainted with the latter instance of my affection yet awhile.

JOSEPH: *(aside)* Nor I, if I could help it.

SIR PETER: *(putting back the papers)* And now, my dear friend, if you please, we will talk over the situation of your hopes with Maria.

JOSEPH: *(in alarm, very softly)* Oh, no, Sir Peter; another time, if you please.

SIR PETER: *(ignoring the objection and speaking emphatically)* I am sensibly chagrined at the little progress you seem to make in her affections.

JOSEPH: *(very quietly, and frantically attempting to change the subject)* I beg you will not mention it. What are my disappointments when your happiness is in debate! *(aside)* 'Sdeath, I shall be ruined every way.

SIR PETER: *(not to be put off)* And though you are so averse to my acquainting Lady Teazle with your passion for Maria, I'm sure she's not your enemy in the affair. *(Lady Teazle appears from behind the screen an instant only in great agitation.)*

JOSEPH: *(speaking rapidly and forcefully)* Pray, Sir Peter, now, oblige me. I am really too much affected by the subject we have been speaking of, to bestow a thought on my own concerns. The man who is intrusted with his friend's distresses can never—*(He is interrupted by the appearance of the servant at the door.)* Well, sir?

SERVANT: Your brother, sir, is speaking to a gentleman in the street, and says he knows you are within.

JOSEPH: *(with angry annoyance)* 'Sdeath, blockhead, I'm not within; I'm out for the day. *(The servant turns to leave.)*

SIR PETER: Stay—hold—a thought has struck me: you shall be at home.

JOSEPH: Well, well, let him up. *(aside as the servant exits)* He'll interrupt Sir Peter, however.

SIR PETER: *(eagerly)* Now, my good friend, oblige me, I entreat you. Before Charles comes, let me conceal myself somewhere; then do you tax him on the point we have been talking, and his answer may satisfy me at once.

JOSEPH: *(pretending to be shocked)* Oh, fie, Sir Peter! would you have me join in so mean a trick?—to trepan my brother, too?

SIR PETER: *(unconsciously employing some of Joseph's own logic)* Nay, you tell me you are sure he is innocent; if so, you do him the greatest service by giving him an opportunity to clear himself, and you will set my heart at rest. Come, you shall not refuse me; *(moving toward the screen)* here, behind this screen will be—*(Joseph catches him by the coat and detains him.)* Hey! what the devil! there seems to be one listener here already. I'll swear I saw a petticoat!

JOSEPH: *(pulling him back as Sir Peter eyes him oddly)* Ha! ha! ha! Well, this is ridiculous enough. I'll tell you, Sir Peter, though I hold a man of intrigue to be a most despicable character, yet, you know, it does not follow that one is to be an absolute Joseph[1] either! Hark'ee, 'tis a little French milliner—a silly rogue that plagues me—and having some character to lose, on your coming, sir, she ran behind the screen.

SIR PETER: *(smiling indulgently)* Ah! you rogue! *(struck by a thought)* But, egad, she has overheard all I have been saying of my wife.

JOSEPH: *(reassuringly and with conscious irony)* Oh, 'twill never go any farther, you may depend upon it.

SIR PETER: No? Then, faith, let her hear it out. *(noticing the closet door at the right)* Here's a closet will do as well.

JOSEPH: Well, go in there.

SIR PETER: *(entering chuckling)* Sly rogue! sly rogue! *(He pulls the door to after him, leaving it slightly ajar.)*

JOSEPH: *(to himself)* A narrow escape, indeed! and a

---

[1] Meaning that he, unlike the Biblical Joseph, will not resist the advances of a woman as Joseph resisted Potiphar's wife.

curious situation I'm in, to part man and wife in this manner.

LADY TEAZLE: *(again peeping around the edge of the screen)* Couldn't I steal off?

JOSEPH: *(in a whisper)* Keep close, my angel!

SIR PETER: *(peering out from behind his door)* Joseph, tax him home.

JOSEPH: *(urgently)* Back, my friend! *(dashes over to close the closet door)*

LADY TEAZLE: *(peeping)* Couldn't you lock Sir Peter in?

JOSEPH: *(with mounting but desperately controlled exasperation)* Be still, my life!

SIR PETER: *(peeping)* You're sure the little milliner won't blab?

JOSEPH: *(in an explosive whisper as he pushes the door shut again)* In, in, my good Sir Peter. *(aside)* 'Fore Gad, I wish I had a key to the door.

Charles breezes in from the left unannounced.

CHARLES: Holloa! brother, what has been the matter? Your fellow would not let me up at first. *(with irritating jocosity)* What! have you had a Jew or a wench with you?

JOSEPH: *(with cold dignity)* Neither, brother, I assure you.

CHARLES: *(looking about the room curiously)* But what has made Sir Peter steal off? I thought he had been with you.

JOSEPH: He *was,* brother; but hearing you were coming, he did not choose to stay.

CHARLES: What! was the old gentleman afraid I wanted to borrow money of him?

JOSEPH: *(in a tone of solemn rebuke but hurrying to the point)* No, sir; but I am sorry to find, Charles, you have lately given that worthy man grounds for great uneasiness.

CHARLES: *(with easy laughter)* Yes, they tell me that I do that to a great many worthy men. *(curious)* But how so, pray?

JOSEPH: To be plain with you, brother, he thinks you are endeavoring to gain Lady Teazle's affections from him.

CHARLES: *(highly amused)* Who, I? Oh, Lud! not I, upon my word. Ha! ha! ha! ha! So the old fellow has found out that he has got a young wife, has he? *(his expression changing to a wry, mocking grin)* Or, what is worse, Lady Teazle has found out she has an old husband?

JOSEPH: *(severely solemn and nervously aware of screen and closet)* This is no subject to jest on, brother. He who can laugh—

CHARLES: *(impatiently depriving screen and closet of the flow of his brother's trite sententiousness)* True, true, as you were going to say—*(soberly)* then, seriously, I never had the least idea of what you charge me with, upon my honor.

JOSEPH: *(raising his voice)* Well, it will give Sir Peter great satisfaction to hear this.

CHARLES: *(with complete light-hearted frankness)* To be sure, I once thought the lady seemed to have taken a fancy to me; but, upon my soul, I never gave her the least encouragement. Besides, you know my attachment to Maria.

JOSEPH: *(by way of emphasizing his own impeccable moral standards)* But sure, brother, even if Lady Teazle had betrayed the fondest partiality for you—

CHARLES: *(sharply, in his abomination of hypocrisy)* Why, look'ee, Joseph, I hope I shall never deliberately do a dishonorable action; but if a pretty woman was purposely to throw herself in my way, and that pretty woman married to a man old enough to be her father—

JOSEPH: *(eagerly awaiting the incriminating conclusion)* Well—

CHARLES: *(laughing easily as he puts his arm around Joseph's shoulder)* Why, I believe I should be obliged to borrow a little of your morality, that's all. *(reflecting)* But, brother, do you know now that you surprise me exceedingly, by naming *me* with Lady Teazle? For, 'faith, I always understood you were her favorite.

JOSEPH: *(vigorously as he scents danger)* Oh, for shame, Charles! This retort is foolish.

CHARLES: *(honestly puzzled)* Nay, I swear I have seen you exchange such significant glances—

JOSEPH: *(cutting him off sternly)* Nay, nay, sir, this is no jest.

CHARLES: Egad, I'm serious. Don't you remember one day when I called here—

JOSEPH: *(throwing up both hands in admonition)* Nay, prithee, Charles—

CHARLES: *(amused now by the reminiscence)* And found you together—

JOSEPH: *(with sharp intensity)* Zounds, sir! I insist—

CHARLES: *(with mounting enthusiasm)* And another time when your servant—

JOSEPH: *(pulling him farther away from the closet)* Brother, brother, a word with you! *(aside)* Gad, I must stop him.

CHARLES: *(oblivious)* Informed, I say, that—

JOSEPH: *(peremptorily)* Hush! *(quietly)* I beg your pardon, but Sir Peter has overheard all we have been saying. I knew you would clear yourself, or I should not have consented.

CHARLES: *(bewildered)* How, Sir Peter! Where is he?

JOSEPH: Softly; there! *(pointing to the closet)*

CHARLES: Oh, 'fore heaven, I'll have him out. Sir Peter come forth!

JOSEPH: No, no—

CHARLES: *(greatly amused but appearing to be highly indignant)* I say, Sir Peter, come into court. *(opening the door and pulling Sir Peter out)* What! my old guardian! *(with mock severity)* What! turn inquisitor, and take evidence incog.?[2]

SIR PETER: *(apologetically)* Give me your hand, Charles. I believe I have suspected you wrongfully; but

---
[2] Incognito.

you mustn't be angry with Joseph. 'Twas my plan!

CHARLES: *(ironically)* Indeed!

SIR PETER: But I acquit you. I promise you I don't think near so ill of you as I did. What I have heard has given me great satisfaction.

CHARLES: Egad, then, 'twas lucky you didn't hear any more! *(to his brother with a parody of the solicitous manner)* Wasn't it, Joseph?

SIR PETER: *(appreciatively)* Ah! you would have retorted on him.

CHARLES: *(easily)* Ay, ay, that was a joke.

SIR PETER: *(convinced from the beginning that it must be)* Yes, yes, I know his honor too well.

CHARLES: But you might as well have suspected *him* as *me* in this matter, for all that. *(to Joseph)* Mightn't he, Joseph?

SIR PETER: *(terminating the discussion)* Well, well, I believe you.

JOSEPH: *(aside)* Would they were both out of the room!

The servant comes in and whispers to Joseph.

SIR PETER: *(observing the servant's entrance and turning confidentially to Charles who has so surprised and pleased him by his straightforward honesty)* And in future perhaps we may not be such strangers.

The servant has delivered his brief message, and leaves.

JOSEPH: Gentlemen, I beg pardon, I must wait on you[3] downstairs; here is a person come on particular business.

CHARLES: Well, you can see him in another room. Sir Peter and I have not met in a long time, and I have something to say to him.

JOSEPH: *(aside)* They must not be left together. *(to his visitors)* I'll send this man away, and return directly. *(apart to Sir Peter)* Sir Peter, not a word of the French milliner.

---

[3] Meaning that he would like to take them to a downstairs room.

SIR PETER: *(apart to Joseph as he leaves)* I! not for the world! *(turning to Charles)* Ah! Charles, if you associated more with your brother, one might indeed hope for your reformation. He is a man of sentiment. Well, there is nothing in the world so noble as a man of sentiment.

CHARLES: Pshaw! he is too moral by half, and so apprehensive of his good name, as he calls it, that I suppose he would as soon let a priest into his house as a girl.

SIR PETER: No! no! come, come! you wrong him. No, no! Joseph is no rake, but he is no such saint either in that respect. *(aside)* I have a great mind to tell him; we should have a laugh at Joseph.

CHARLES: Oh, hang him! He's a very anchorite, a young hermit.

SIR PETER: Hark'ee, you must not abuse him; he may chance hear of it again, I promise you.

CHARLES: *(mystified)* Why, *you* won't tell him?

SIR PETER: No—but—this way. *(aside as he guides him toward the screen)* Egad, I'll tell him. *(slyly to Charles)* Hark'ee, have you a mind to have a good laugh at Joseph?

CHARLES: I should like it of all things.

SIR PETER: Then, i'faith, we will; I'll be quit with him for discovering me. He had a girl with him when I called.

CHARLES: *(incredulous and delighted with the paradox)* What! Joseph? You jest.

SIR PETER: Hush! a little French milliner, and the best of the jest is, she's in the room now. *(chuckling and pointing toward the screen)*

CHARLES: The devil she is!

SIR PETER: Hush! I tell you! *(points directly at the screen)*

CHARLES: Behind the screen! 'Slife, let's unveil her!

SIR PETER: *(hearing footsteps outside)* No, no—he's coming—you shan't indeed!

CHARLES: *(advancing toward the screen in high good humor)* Oh, egad, we'll have a peep at the little milliner!

SIR PETER: *(with trepidation—holding him back)* Not for the world; Joseph will never forgive me—

CHARLES: *(gaily)* I'll stand by you— *(reaches for the screen)*

SIR PETER: *(seeing Joseph about to enter)* Odds, here he is.

Joseph enters just as Charles throws down the screen, revealing Lady Teazle. Charles and Sir Peter step back in utter amazement!

CHARLES: *(gulping with mingled wonder and amazement)* Lady Teazle, by all that's wonderful!

SIR PETER: *(thunderstruck)* Lady Teazle, by all that's damnable!

CHARLES: *(inwardly delighted, with mock seriousness)* Sir Peter, this is one of the smartest French milliners I ever saw. Egad, you seem all to have been diverting yourselves here at hide and seek, and I don't see who is out of the secret. Shall I beg your ladyship to inform me? Not a word! Brother, will you be pleased to explain this matter? What! Is Morality dumb too? Sir Peter, though I found you in the dark, perhaps you are not so now! All mute! Well, though I can make nothing of the affair, I suppose you perfectly understand one another, so I'll leave you to yourselves. *(bowing to Joseph in leave-taking)* Brother, I'm sorry to find you have given that worthy man cause for so much uneasiness. *(to Sir Peter)* Sir Peter! there's nothing in the world so noble as a man of sentiment!

Charles exits with a flourish as the others stand for some time looking at each other.

JOSEPH: *(attempting to palliate the shock, in a hesitating voice)* Sir Peter—notwithstanding—I confess—that appearances are against me—if you will afford me your patience—I make no doubt—but I shall explain everything to your satisfaction.

SIR PETER: *(icily)* If you please, sir.

JOSEPH: *(still inarticulate, fumbling for words, and with barely a trace of his usual suave manner)* The fact

is, sir, that Lady Teazle, knowing my pretensions to your ward Maria—I say, sir, Lady Teazle, being apprehensive of the jealousy of your temper—and knowing my friendship to the family—she, sir, I say—called here—in order that—I might explain these pretensions—but on your coming—being apprehensive—as I said—of your jealousy—she withdrew—and this, you may depend on it, is the whole truth of the matter.

SIR PETER: *(with heavy sarcasm)* A very clear account, upon my word; and I dare swear the lady will vouch for every article of it.

LADY TEAZLE: *(thoroughly disgusted with the whole situation, including her own part in it)* For not one word of it, Sir Peter!

SIR PETER: How! don't you think it worth while to agree in the lie.

LADY TEAZLE: *(with clear, open betrayal of the alliance)* There is not one syllable of truth in what that gentleman has told you.

SIR PETER: *(heavily)* I believe you, upon my soul, ma'am!

JOSEPH: *(aside to Lady Teazle)* 'Sdeath, madam, will you betray me?

LADY TEAZLE: *(sharply and beginning to assume a virtuous tone)* Good Mr. Hypocrite, by your leave, I'll speak for myself.

SIR PETER: Ay, let her alone, sir; you'll find she'll make out a better story than you, without prompting.

LADY TEAZLE: *(with somewhat ambiguous frankness)* Hear me, Sir Peter! I came hither on no matter relating to your ward, and even ignorant of this gentleman's pretensions to her. But I came seduced by his insidious arguments, *(with ascending virtuousness)* at least to listen to his pretended passion, if not to sacrifice your honor to his baseness.

SIR PETER: Now, I believe, the truth is coming indeed!

JOSEPH: *(weakly)* The woman's mad!

LADY TEAZLE: *(bursting the floodgates of her repressed feelings)* No, sir, she has recovered her senses, and your own arts have furnished her with the means. Sir Peter, I do not expect you to credit me, but the tenderness you expressed for me, when I am sure you could not think I was a witness to it, has penetrated so to my heart, that had I left the place without the shame of this discovery, my future life should have spoken the sincerity of my gratitude. As for that smooth-tongued hypocrite, who would have seduced the wife of his too credulous friend, while he affected honorable addresses to his ward, I behold him now in a light so truly despicable, that I shall never again respect myself for having listened to him. *(She rushes from the room on the verge of tears.)*

JOSEPH: *(regaining his self-possession and speaking in his customary manner)* Notwithstanding all this, Sir Peter, Heaven knows—

SIR PETER: *(interrupting vehemently)* That you are a villain! and so I leave you to your conscience. *(turns without ceremony and strides off after his wife.)*

JOSEPH: *(protesting vigorously as he follows him out)* You are too rash, Sir Peter; you shall hear me. The man who shuts out conviction by refusing to—*(The remainder of his "sentiment" is lost to the audience as he leaves the stage to pursue Sir Peter.)*

ACT FIVE

Scene One

The Library in Joseph Surface's house. Joseph enters through the wings from the right in conversation with a servant, angrily rebuking him.

JOSEPH: Mr. Stanley! And why should you think I would see him? You must know he comes to ask for something.

SERVANT: Sir, I should not have let him in, but that Mr. Rowley came to the door with him.

JOSEPH: *(out of patience)* Pshaw! blockhead! to suppose that I should now be in a temper to receive visits from poor relations! Well, why don't you show the fellow up?

SERVANT: I will, sir. *(protesting)* Why, sir, it was not my fault that Sir Peter discovered my lady—

JOSEPH: *(cutting him off irritably)* Go, fool! *(The servant retires to the left)* Sure Fortune never played a man of my policy such a trick before. My character with Sir Peter, my hopes with Maria, destroyed in a moment! I'm in a rare humor to listen to other people's distresses! I shan't be able to bestow even a benevolent sentiment on Stanley. *(looking toward the left)* So! here he comes, and Rowley with him. I must try to recover myself, and put a little charity into my face, however. *(He leaves hurriedly to the right.)*

Sir Oliver Surface and Rowley enter just as Joseph vanishes.

SIR OLIVER: *(looking after the departing figure)* What! does he avoid us? That was he, was it not?

ROWLEY: *(with the barest hint of sarcasm)* It was, sir. But I doubt you are come a little too abruptly. His nerves are so weak that the sight of a poor relation may be too much for him. I should have gone first to break it to him.

SIR OLIVER: *(impatiently)* Oh, plague of his nerves! *(with wonderment)* Yet this is he whom Sir Peter extols as a man of the most benevolent way of thinking!

ROWLEY: *(abandoning any effort to conceal his true feelings)* As to his way of thinking, I cannot pretend to decide; for, to do him justice, he appears to have as much speculative benevolence as any private gentleman in the kingdom, though he is seldom so sensual as to indulge himself in the exercise of it.

SIR OLIVER: Yet has a string of charitable sentiments at his fingers' ends.

ROWLEY: Or rather at his tongue's end, Sir Oliver; for I believe there is no sentiment he has such faith in, as that "Charity begins at home."

SIR OLIVER: *(agreeing, and adding to Rowley's whimsical analysis)* And his, I presume, is of that domestic sort which never stirs abroad at all?

ROWLEY: I doubt you'll find it so—but he's coming. I mustn't seem to interrupt you; and, you know, immediately as you leave him, I come in to announce your arrival in your real character.

SIR OLIVER: True; and afterwards you'll meet me at Sir Peter's.

ROWLEY: *(going)* Without losing a moment. *(He leaves.)*

SIR OLIVER: *(ruminatively, as he sees Joseph about to enter)* I don't like the complaisance of his features.

JOSEPH: *(coming in—again the finished actor)* Sir, I beg you ten thousand pardons for keeping you a moment waiting. Mr. Stanley, I presume.

SIR OLIVER: *(deferentially)* At your service.

JOSEPH: *(solicitously and with suspiciously elaborate civility)* Sir, I beg you will do me the honor to sit down. I entreat you, sir!

SIR OLIVER: Dear sir, there's no occasion. *(aside)* Too civil by half!

JOSEPH: *(smoothly)* I have not the pleasure of knowing you, Mr. Stanley, but I am extremely happy to see you look so well. You were nearly related to my mother, I think, Mr. Stanley?

SIR OLIVER: *(picking up Joseph's style)* I was, sir; so nearly, that my present poverty, I fear, may do discredit to her wealthy children, else I should not have presumed to trouble you.

JOSEPH: *(expansively and gracefully parrying the thrust with gently melancholic countenance)* Dear sir, there needs no apology; he that is in distress, though a stranger, has a right to claim kindred with the wealthy. I am sure I wish I was of that class, and had it in my power to offer you even a small relief.

SIR OLIVER: *(simulating a faint sigh)* If your uncle, Sir Oliver, were here, I should have a friend.

JOSEPH: *(with equally simulated warmth)* I wish he was, sir, with all my heart: you should not want an advocate with him, believe me, sir.

SIR OLIVER: I should not need one—my distresses would recommend me. *(with directness)* But I imagined his bounty would enable you to become the agent of his charity.

JOSEPH: *(in gentle reproof of so erring an impression)* My dear sir, you were strangely misinformed. *(in a tone of stoical acceptance of the injustices of life)* Sir Oliver is a worthy man, a very worthy man; but avarice, Mr. Stanley, is the vice of age. I will tell you, my good sir, in confidence, what he has done for me has been a mere nothing; though people, I know, have thought otherwise, and, for my part, I never chose to contradict the report.

SIR OLIVER: What! has he never transmitted you bullion—rupees—pagodas?[1]

JOSEPH: *(with patient forbearance)* Oh, dear sir, nothing of the kind! No, no; a few presents, now and then—

---

[1] Silver and gold Indian coins.

china, shawls, congou tea, avadavats, and Indian crackers;[2] little more, believe me.

SIR OLIVER: *(aside)* Here's gratitude for twelve thousand pounds! Avadavats and Indian crackers!

JOSEPH: *(warming to his theme)* Then, my dear sir, you have heard, I doubt not, of the extravagance of my brother; there are very few would credit what I have done for that unfortunate young man.

SIR OLIVER: *(aside)* Not I, for one!

JOSEPH: *(in an elegiac tone of mock remorse)* The sums I have lent him! Indeed I have been exceedingly to blame; it was an amiable weakness. However, I don't pretend to defend it; and now I feel doubly culpable, since it has deprived me of the pleasure of serving you, Mr. Stanley, as my heart dictates.

SIR OLIVER: *(aside)* Dissembler! *(to Joseph, in a crushed tone)* Then, sir, you can't assist me?

JOSEPH: *(exuding sympathy)* At present, it grieves me to say, I cannot; but, whenever I have the ability, you may depend upon hearing from me.

SIR OLIVER: *(weakly)* I am extremely sorry—

JOSEPH: *(drowning him out with fastidious insincerity)* Not more than I, believe me; to pity without the power to relieve, is still more painful than to ask and be denied.

SIR OLIVER: *(bowing low in leave-taking)* Kind sir, your most obedient humble servant.

JOSEPH: *(sorrowfully, yet grandly, as though conferring a great favor)* You leave me deeply affected, Mr. Stanley. *(calling to the servant)* William, be ready to open the door.

SIR OLIVER: *(humbly but with barely concealed irritation)* Oh, dear sir, no ceremony.

JOSEPH: *(bowing slightly)* Your very obedient.

SIR OLIVER: *(with a very deep bow)* Sir, your most obsequious .

JOSEPH: *(cheerfully)* You may depend upon hearing from me, whenever I can be of service.

---

[2] Black Chinese tea, songbirds, and firecrackers.

SIR OLIVER: *(seemingly overwhelmed)* Sweet sir, you are too good!

JOSEPH: *(retaining his solicitous air but almost betraying his joy at Mr. Stanley's retreat)* In the meantime I wish you health and spirits.

SIR OLIVER: *(with a final bow and a voice of ringing sincerity)* Your ever grateful and perpetual humble servant.

JOSEPH: *(deeply affected, and returning the bow)* Sir, yours as sincerely.

SIR OLIVER: *(aside, explosively, as he turns and goes through the door)* Charles, you are my heir!

JOSEPH: *(alone—with wry and sober amusement at his own impersonations)* This is one bad effect of a good character; it invites application from the unfortunate, and there needs no small degree of address to gain the reputation of benevolence without incurring the expense. The silver ore of pure charity is an expensive article in the catalogue of a man's good qualities; whereas the sentimental French plate I use instead of it, makes just as good a show, and pays no tax.

Rowley enters unannounced.

ROWLEY: *(apologetically)* Mr. Surface, your servant. I was apprehensive of interrupting you, though my business demands immediate attention, as this note will inform you.

JOSEPH: *(taking the note; abstractedly)* Always happy to see Mr. Rowley. *(glancing at its contents)* How! *(surprised by the signature)* "Oliver Surface!" My uncle arrived!

ROWLEY: He is, indeed; we have just parted—quite well, after a speedy voyage, and impatient to embrace his worthy nephew.

JOSEPH: I am astonished. *(calling to the servant)* William! stop Mr. Stanley, if he's not gone.

ROWLEY: *(inwardly amused)* Oh! he's out of reach, I believe.

JOSEPH: *(irritability supplanting his courtly hospital-*

ity) Why did you not let me know this when you came in together?

ROWLEY: I thought you had particular business; but I must be gone to inform your brother, and appoint him here to meet your uncle. He will be with you in a quarter of an hour.

JOSEPH: *(looking at the note)* So he says. *(solemnly)* Well, I am strangely overjoyed at his coming. *(aside)* Never, to be sure, was anything so damned unlucky.

ROWLEY: *(starting to go)* You will be delighted to see how well he looks.

JOSEPH: Ah! I'm rejoiced to hear it. *(aside)* Just at this time!

ROWLEY: *(leaving)* I'll tell him how impatiently you expect him.

JOSEPH: *(seeing him)* Do, do; pray give my best duty and affection. Indeed, I cannot express the sensations I feel at the thought of seeing him. *(turning back for a moment)* Certainly his coming at this time is the cruelest piece of ill fortune! *(He goes out after Rowley.)*

Scene Two

The Parlor of Sir Peter Teazle's house to which the clan is drawn by the magnet of the already widespread gossip concerning Sir Peter's discovery of his young wife in Joseph Surface's library.

Mrs. Candour, the first caller, enters from the outer hall at the left, brushing aside the protests of Sir Peter's maid who has admitted her.

MAID: Indeed, ma'am, my lady will see nobody at present.

MRS. CANDOUR: Did you tell her it was her friend Mrs. Candour?

MAID: Yes, ma'am; but she begs you will excuse her.

MRS. CANDOUR: *(with overwhelming confidence)* Do go again; I shall be glad to see her, if it be only for a moment, for I am sure she must be in great distress. *(grumbling to herself as the maid leaves)* Dear heart, how provoking! I'm not mistress of half the circumstances! We shall have the whole affair in the newspapers, with the names of the parties at length, before I have dropped the story at a dozen houses. *(turns to perceive the entrance of Sir Benjamin Backbite)* Oh, Sir Benjamin, you have heard, I suppose—

SIR BENJAMIN: *(pleased that he can anticipate the conclusion of her sentence)* Of Lady Teazle and Mr. Surface—

MRS. CANDOUR: *(determined to be first on at least one item)* And Sir Peter's discovery—

SIR BENJAMIN: Oh! the strangest bit of business, to be sure!

MRS. CANDOUR: Well, I never was so surprised in my life. I am so sorry for all parties, indeed.

SIR BENJAMIN: Now, I don't pity Sir Peter at all; he was so extravagantly partial of Mr. Surface.

MRS. CANDOUR: *(surprised)* Mr. Surface! Why, 'twas with Charles Lady Teazle was detected.

SIR BENJAMIN: *(with condescending superiority)* No, no, I tell you; Mr. Surface is the gallant.

MRS. CANDOUR: *(irritated)* No such thing! Charles is the man. 'Twas Mr. Surface brought Sir Peter on purpose to discover them.

SIR BENJAMIN: *(patiently)* I tell you I had it from one—

MRS. CANDOUR: *(her temper rising)* And I have it from one—

SIR BENJAMIN: *(ignoring the interruption)* Who had it from one, who had it—

MRS. CANDOUR: *(with angry finality)* From one immediately—*(cutting herself off sharply as she sees Lady Sneerwell about to enter. Her tone changes to a mellifluous coo.)* —but here comes Lady Sneerwell; perhaps she knows the whole affair.

Lady Sneerwell enters.

LADY SNEERWELL: *(concealing her excited enthusiasm*

beneath a half-sigh of funereal compassion) So, my dear Mrs. Candour, here's a sad affair of our friend, Lady Teazle.

MRS. CANDOUR: *(replying in kind)* Ay, my dear friend, who would have thought—

LADY SNEERWELL: *(dropping the pretense)* Well, there is no trusting appearances; though, indeed, she was always too lively for me.

MRS. CANDOUR: *(as if not wishing to speak unkindly of the deceased)* To be sure, her manners were a little too free; but then she was so young!

LADY SNEERWELL: *(wanting to be just)* And had, indeed, some good qualities.

MRS. CANDOUR: So she had, indeed. But have you heard the particulars?

LADY SNEERWELL: No; but everybody says that Mr. Surface—

SIR BENJAMIN: *(triumphantly)* Ay, there; I told you Mr. Surface was the man.

MRS. CANDOUR: No, no; indeed the assignation was with Charles.

LADY SNEERWELL: *(betraying her own interest in him)* With Charles! You alarm me, Mrs. Candour!

MRS. CANDOUR: *(with certainty)* Yes, yes, he was the lover. Mr. Surface, to do him justice, was only the informer.

SIR BENJAMIN: Well, I'll not dispute with you, Mrs. Candour; but, be it which it may, I hope that Sir Peter's wound will not—

MRS. CANDOUR: Sir Peter's wound! Oh, mercy! I didn't hear a word of their fighting.

LADY SNEERWELL: Nor I, a syllable.

SIR BENJAMIN: No! what, no mention of the duel?

MRS. CANDOUR: Not a word.

SIR BENJAMIN: Oh, yes; they fought before they left the room.

LADY SNEERWELL: *(avidly)* Pray, let us hear.

MRS. CANDOUR: *(chiming in)* Ay, do oblige us with the duel.

SIR BENJAMIN: *(assuming a dramatic pose)* "Sir," says Sir Peter, immediately after the discovery, "you are a most ungrateful fellow."

MRS. CANDOUR: *(determined to needle Lady Sneerwell)* Ay, to Charles.

SIR BENJAMIN: *(annoyed at the interruption)* No, no, to Mr. Surface. *(resuming his theatrical tone)* "—a most ungrateful fellow; and, old as I am, sir," says he, "I insist on immediate satisfaction."

MRS. CANDOUR: Ay, that must have been to Charles; for 'tis very unlikely that Mr. Surface should fight in his own house.

SIR BENJAMIN: *(brushing aside her remark)* Gad's life, ma'am, not at all. *(continuing)* "—giving me immediate satisfaction." On this, ma'am, Lady Teazle, seeing Sir Peter in such danger, ran out of the room in strong hysterics, and Charles after her, calling out for hartshorn and water; then, madam, they began to fight with swords.

Crabtree has entered during the last part of Sir Benjamin's vivid account, but the rapt attention of the little group has permitted no notice of his arrival.

CRABTREE: *(testily)* With pistols, nephew—pistols. I have it from undoubted authority.

MRS. CANDOUR: Oh, Mr. Crabtree, then it is all true!

CRABTREE: *(sorrowfully)* Too true, indeed, madam, and Sir Peter is dangerously wounded—

SIR BENJAMIN: By a thrust in *seconde*[1] quite through his left side—

CRABTREE: *(firmly)* By a bullet lodged in the thorax.

MRS. CANDOUR: *(with exquisitely gratified horror)* Mercy on me! Poor Sir Peter!

CRABTREE: Yes, madam; though Charles would have avoided the matter, if he could.

MRS. CANDOUR: I knew Charles was the person.

SIR BENJAMIN: *(with a superior air)* My uncle, I see, knows nothing of the matter.

---

[1] Using a fencing term to contradict his uncle's version of the fight.

CRABTREE: *(ignoring him)* But Sir Peter taxed him with the basest ingratitude.

SIR BENJAMIN: *That* I told you, you know—

CRABTREE: *(his voice rising)* Do, nephew, let me speak! - -and insisted on immediate—

SIR BENJAMIN: *Just* as I said—

CRABTREE: *(shouting)* Odds life, nephew, allow others to know something too! A pair of pistols lay on the bureau (for Mr. Surface, it seems, had come home the night before from Salthill, where he had been to see the Montem[2] with a friend who has a son at Eton), so, unluckily, the pistols were left charged.

SIR BENJAMIN: *(taken back)* I heard nothing of this.

CRABTREE: *(with mounting assurance)* Sir Peter forced Charles to take one, and they fired, it seems, pretty nearly together. Charles's shot took effect, as I tell you, and Sir Peter's missed; but what is very extraordinary, the ball struck against a little bronze Shakespeare that stood over the fireplace, grazed out of the window, at a right angle, and wounded the postman, who was just coming to the door with a double letter[3] from Northamptonshire.

SIR BENJAMIN: *(annoyed at having lost the limelight)* My uncle's account is more circumstantial, I confess; but I believe mine is the true one, for all that.

LADY SNEERWELL: *(aside)* I am more interested in this affair than they imagine, and must have better information. *(She goes out quietly to the left to call on Charles.)*

SIR BENJAMIN: Ah! Lady Sneerwell's alarm is very easily accounted for.

CRABTREE: Yes, yes, they certainly do say; but that's neither here nor there.

MRS. CANDOUR: But, pray, where is Sir Peter at present?

---

[2] A traditional school ceremony; he had carried loaded pistols because night travel was not considered safe.

[3] A heavy letter requiring extra postage.

CRABTREE: Oh! they brought him home, and he is now in the house, though the servants are ordered to deny him.

MRS. CANDOUR: I believe so, and Lady Teazle, I suppose, attending him.

CRABTREE: Yes, yes; and I saw one of the faculty[4] enter just before me.

SIR BENJAMIN: *(perceiving a stranger about to enter)* Hey, who comes here?

CRABTREE: Oh, this is he: the physician, depend on't.

MRS. CANDOUR: Oh, certainly: it must be the physician; and now we shall know.

Sir Oliver Surface enters. They cluster about him.

CRABTREE: Well, doctor, what hopes?

MRS. CANDOUR: Ah, doctor, how's your patient?

SIR BENJAMIN: Now, doctor, isn't it a wound with a small-sword?

CRABTREE: *(willing to bet on his version of the duel)* A bullet lodged in the thorax, for a hundred!

SIR OLIVER: *(completely at a loss)* Doctor! a wound with a small-sword! and a bullet in the thorax! Oons! are you mad, good people?

SIR BENJAMIN: Perhaps, sir, you are not a doctor?

SIR OLIVER: Truly, I am to thank you for my degree, if I am.

CRABTREE: Only a friend of Sir Peter's, then, I presume. But, sir, you must have heard of his accident?

SIR OLIVER: Not a word!

CRABTREE: Not of his being dangerously wounded?

SIR OLIVER: The devil he is!

SIR BENJAMIN: Run through the body—

CRABTREE: Shot in the breast—

SIR BENJAMIN: By one Mr. Surface—

CRABTREE: Ay, the younger.

SIR OLIVER: *(shutting off the flood of jabberings)* Hey! what the plague! you seem to differ strangely in your accounts: however, you agree that Sir Peter is dangerously wounded.

---

4 Medical profession.

SIR BENJAMIN: Oh, yes, we agree there.

CRABTREE: Yes, yes, I believe there can be no doubt of that.

SIR OLIVER: *(looking toward the right wings)* Then, upon my word, for a person in that situation, he is the most imprudent man alive; for here he comes, walking as if nothing at all was the matter. *(Sir Peter enters, looking generally unhappy)* Odds heart, Sir Peter, you are come in good time, I promise you; for we had just given you over.

SIR BENJAMIN: *(in amazement)* Egad, uncle, this is the most sudden recovery!

SIR OLIVER: *(enjoying the situation enormously)* Why, man, what do you out of bed with a small-sword through your body, and a bullet lodged in your thorax?

SIR PETER: *(bewildered)* A small-sword, and a bullet!

SIR OLIVER: Ay, these gentlemen would have killed you without law or physic, and wanted to dub me a doctor, to make me an accomplice.

SIR PETER: Why, what is all this?

SIR BENJAMIN: *(piously)* We rejoice, Sir Peter, that the story of the duel is not true, and are sincerely sorry for your other misfortune.

SIR PETER: *(aside)* So, so; all over the town already.

CRABTREE: *(rebuking him gently)* Though, Sir Peter, you were certainly vastly to blame to marry at your years.

SIR PETER: *(sharply)* Sir, what business is that of yours?

MRS. CANDOUR: *(sympathetically)* Though, indeed, as Sir Peter made so good a husband, he's very much to be pitied.

SIR PETER: *(testily)* Plague on your pity, ma'am! I desire none of it.

SIR BENJAMIN: *(as if to bolster his morale)* However, Sir Peter, you must not mind the laughing and jests you will meet with on this occasion.

SIR PETER: *(addressing himself to the two men in turn)* Sir, sir, I desire to be master in my own house.

CRABTREE: *(ignoring the hint and piling on the bogus sympathy)* 'Tis no uncommon case, that's one comfort.

SIR PETER: *(with cold firmness)* I insist on being left to myself; without ceremony. I insist on your leaving my house directly.

MRS. CANDOUR: *(showing her disgust at this insulting treatment)* Well, well, we are going, and depend on't we'll make the best report of it we can. *(She sweeps out.)*

SIR PETER: *(to Crabtree)* Leave my house!

CRABTREE: *(bowing and turning to go, with exaggerated sympathy)* And tell how hardly you've been treated.

SIR PETER: *(to Sir Benjamin)* Leave my house!

SIR BENJAMIN: *(mimicking his uncle as he follows him out the door)* And how patiently you bear it.

SIR PETER: *(exploding to Sir Oliver)* Fiends, vipers, furies! Oh! that their own venom would choke them!

SIR OLIVER: They are very provoking, indeed, Sir Peter.

Rowley enters with an inquiring expression on his face.

ROWLEY: *(to Sir Peter)* I heard high words. What has ruffled you, sir?

SIR PETER: Pshaw! what signifies asking? Do I ever pass a day without my vexations?

ROWLEY: *(gently)* Well, I'm not inquisitive.

SIR OLIVER: *(as if disposing of the recent unpleasantness and getting down to the purpose of his call)* Well, Sir Peter, I have seen both my nephews in the manner we proposed.

SIR PETER: *(still deeply rankled)* A precious couple they are!

ROWLEY: Yes, and Sir Oliver is convinced that your judgment was right, Sir Peter.

SIR OLIVER: *(decisively)* Yes, I find Joseph is indeed the man, after all.

ROWLEY: *(joining the plot to bait Sir Peter)* Ay, as Sir Peter says, he is a man of sentiment.

SIR OLIVER: And acts up to the sentiments he professes.

I insist on your leaving my house directly.

ROWLEY: It certainly is edification to hear him talk.

SIR OLIVER: Oh, he's a model for the young men of the age! But how's this, Sir Peter? You don't join us in your friend Joseph's praise, as I expected.

SIR PETER: *(glumly)* Sir Oliver, we live in a damned wicked world, and the fewer we praise the better.

ROWLEY: What! do you say so, Sir Peter, who were never mistaken in your life?

SIR PETER: *(exploding again)* Pshaw! Plague on you both! I see by your sneering you have heard the whole affair. *(shouting)* I shall go mad among you!

ROWLEY: *(with sincerity)* Then, to fret you no longer, Sir Peter, we are indeed acquainted with it all. I met Lady Teazle coming from Mr. Surface's so humbled that she deigned to request me to be her advocate with you.

SIR PETER: And does Sir Oliver know all this?

SIR OLIVER: *(with a trace of a smile)* Every circumstance.

SIR PETER: What! of the closet and the screen, hey?

SIR OLIVER: *(hilariously)* Yes, yes, and the little French milliner. Oh, I have been vastly diverted with the story! Ha! ha! ha!

SIR PETER: *(drily)* 'Twas very pleasant.

SIR OLIVER: I never laughed more in my life, I assure you. Ha! ha! ha!

SIR PETER: Oh, vastly diverting! *(bitterly)* Ha! ha! ha!

ROWLEY: *(joining in the mirth)* To be sure, Joseph with his sentiments! Ha! ha! ha!

SIR PETER: *(hollowly)* Yes, yes, his sentiments! Ha! ha! ha! *(furiously)* Hypocritical villain!

SIR OLIVER: *(delighted)* Ay, and that rogue Charles to pull Sir Peter out of the closet: ha! ha! ha!

SIR PETER: *(with an air of patient martyrdom)* Ha! ha! 'twas devilish entertaining, to be sure!

SIR OLIVER: *(almost choking with laughter)* Ha! ha! ha! Egad, Sir Peter, I should like to have seen your face when the screen was thrown down: ha! ha!

SIR PETER: *(mechanically)* Yes, yes, my face when the

screen was thrown down: ha! ha! ha! *(in anguish)* Oh, I must never show my head again!

SIR OLIVER: *(making a strenuous attempt to be sober)* But come, come, it isn't fair to laugh at you neither, my old friend; *(nearly going off again)* though, upon my soul, I can't help it.

SIR PETER: *(sarcastically)* Oh, pray don't restrain your mirth on my account; it does not hurt me at all! I laugh at the whole affair myself. Yes, yes, I think being a standing jest for all one's acquaintance a very happy situation. Oh, yes, and then of a morning to read the paragraphs about Mr. S——, Lady T——, and Sir P—— will be so entertaining.

ROWLEY: *(seriously)* Without affectation, Sir Peter, you may despise the ridicule of fools—*(looking offstage to the right)* but I see Lady Teazle going towards the next room. I am sure you must desire a reconciliation as earnestly as she does.

SIR OLIVER: *(in a sincerely friendly tone)* Perhaps my being here prevents her coming to you. Well, I'll leave honest Rowley to meditate between you; but he must bring you all presently to Mr. Surface's, where I am now returning, if not to reclaim a libertine, at least to expose hypocrisy.

SIR PETER: *(recovering his spirits)* Ah, I'll be present at your discovering yourself there with all my heart; *(wryly)* though 'tis a vile unlucky place for discoveries!

ROWLEY: *(to Sir Oliver as he goes out to the left)* We'll follow.

SIR PETER: *(turning to Rowley)* She is not coming here, you see, Rowley.

ROWLEY: No, but she has left the door of that room open, you perceive. *(nodding toward the right wings)* See, she is in tears.

SIR PETER: *(inwardly melting)* Certainly a little mortification appears very becoming in a wife. Don't you think it will do her good to let her pine a little?

ROWLEY: *(gently)* Oh, this is ungenerous in you!

SIR PETER: Well, I know what to think. You remember the letter I found of hers, evidently intended for Charles?

ROWLEY: A mere forgery, Sir Peter, laid in your way on purpose. This is one of the points which I intend Snake shall give you conviction of.

SIR PETER: *(won over)* I wish I were once satisfied of that. She looks this way. What a remarkably elegant turn of the head she has! *(with happy decision)* Rowley, I'll go to her.

ROWLEY: *(encouragingly)* Certainly.

SIR PETER: *(hesitating)* Though when it is known that we are reconciled, people will laugh at me ten times more.

ROWLEY: *(heartily)* Let them laugh, and retort their malice only by showing them you are happy in spite of it.

SIR PETER: *(his face lighting up)* I'faith, so I will! And if I'm not mistaken, we may be the happiest couple in the country.

ROWLEY: *(unable to forbear a last teazing reminder of Sir Peter's miscalculation of Joseph's character; imitating Joseph's voice and manner)* Nay, Sir Peter, he who once lays aside suspicion—

SIR PETER: *(shutting him off abruptly and with vehemence)* Hold, Master Rowley! if you have any regard for me, let me never hear you utter anything like a sentiment. I have had enough of them to serve me the rest of my life.

They exchange smiles of mutual understanding and leave in opposite directions, Rowley to follow Sir Oliver to Joseph Surface's and Sir Peter to seek out his wife.

Scene Three

The Library in Joseph Surface's house. Joseph Surface enters from the left with Lady Sneerwell who is talking heatedly.

LADY SNEERWELL: Impossible! Will not Sir Peter immediately be reconciled to Charles, and, of course, no longer oppose his union with Maria? The thought is distraction to me.

JOSEPH: *(coldly)* Can passion furnish a remedy?

LADY SNEERWELL: No, nor cunning neither. Oh! I was a fool, an idiot, to league with such a blunderer!

JOSEPH: *(ignoring the accusation)* Sure, Lady Sneerwell, *I* am the greatest sufferer; yet you see I bear the accident with calmness.

LADY SNEERWELL: *(bitterly)* Because the disappointment doesn't reach your heart; your interest only attached you to Maria. Had you felt for her what I have for that ungrateful libertine, neither your temper nor hypocrisy could prevent your showing the sharpness of your vexation.

JOSEPH: *(self-righteously)* But why should your reproaches fall on me for this disappointment?

LADY SNEERWELL: *(angrily)* Are you not the cause of it? Had you not a sufficient field for your roguery in imposing upon Sir Peter, and supplanting your brother, but you must endeavor to seduce his wife? I hate such an avarice of crimes; 'tis an unfair monopoly, and never prospers.

JOSEPH: *(smoothly)* Well, I admit I have been to blame. I confess I deviated from the direct road of wrong, but I don't think we're so totally defeated neither.

LADY SNEERWELL: *(highly skeptical)* No!

JOSEPH: You tell me you have made a trial of Snake since we met, and that you still believe him faithful to us —

LADY SNEERWELL: I do believe so.

JOSEPH: *(carefully setting forth the plan)* And that he has undertaken, should it be necessary, to swear and prove that Charles is at this time contracted by vows and honor to your ladyship, which some of his former letters to you will serve to support?

LADY SNEERWELL: *(uncertainly)* This, indeed, might have assisted.

JOSEPH: *(as if soothing a petulant child)* Come, come;

it is not too late yet. *(There is a knock at the outside door.)* But hark! this is probably my uncle, Sir Oliver. Retire to that room *(pointing to the door at the right)*; we'll consult farther when he is gone.

LADY SNEERWELL: *(dubious)* Well, but if *he* should find you out too?

JOSEPH: *(exuding confidence)* Oh, I have no fear of that. Sir Peter will hold his tongue for his own credit's sake; and you may depend on it I shall soon discover Sir Oliver's weak side!

LADY SNEERWELL: *(retiring to the room indicated)* I have no diffidence of your abilities! Only be constant to one roguery at a time. *(She goes out, closing the door behind her.)*

JOSEPH: *(alone, peering toward the left)* I will, I will. So! 'tis confounded hard, after such bad fortune, to be baited by one's confederate in evil. Well, at all events, my character is so much better than Charles's, that I certainly—hey!—what!—this is not Sir Oliver, but old Stanley again. Plague on't that he should return to tease me just now! I shall have Sir Oliver come and find him here—and— *(Sir Oliver walks in.)* Gad's life, Mr. Stanley, why have you come back to plague me at this time? You must not stay now, upon my word.

SIR OLIVER: Sir, I hear your uncle Oliver is expected here, and though he has been so penurious to you, I'll try what he'll do for me.

JOSEPH: *(urgently)* Sir, 'tis impossible for you to stay now, so I must beg—come any other time, and I promise you, you shall be assisted.

SIR OLIVER: *(with firmness)* No; Sir Oliver and I must be acquainted.

JOSEPH: Zounds, sir! then I insist on your quitting the room directly.

SIR OLIVER: Nay, sir—

JOSEPH: *(moving toward him belligerently)* Sir, I insist on't: here, William! show this gentleman out. Since you compel me, sir, not one moment; this is such insolence! *(Not waiting for the servant, he starts to push Sir Oliver out just as Charles appears.)*

CHARLES: Hey day! what's the matter now! What the devil, have you got hold of my little broker here? Zounds, brother! don't hurt little Premium. *(to Sir Oliver)* What's the matter, my little fellow?

JOSEPH: So! he has been with you too, has he?

CHARLES: To be sure that. Why, he's as honest a little —*(struck by a surprising thought)* But sure, Joseph, you have not been borrowing money too, have you?

JOSEPH: *(not comprehending)* Borrowing! no! But, brother, you know we expect Sir Oliver here every—

CHARLES: Oh, Gad, that's true! Noll mustn't find the little broker here, to be sure.

JOSEPH: Yet Mr. Stanley insists—

CHARLES: Stanley! why, his name's Premium.

JOSEPH: No, sir, Stanley.

CHARLES: No, no, Premium.

JOSEPH: Well, no matter which—but—

CHARLES: Ay, ay, Stanley or Premium, 'tis the same thing, as you say; for I suppose he goes by half a hundred names, besides A.B.[1] at the coffee-house. *(Another knock is heard at the outside door.)*

JOSEPH: 'Sdeath, here's Sir Oliver at the door. Now I beg, Mr. Stanley—

CHARLES: Ay, ay, and I beg, Mr. Premium—

SIR OLIVER: *(standing firm)* Gentlemen—

JOSEPH: Sir, by heaven you shall go!

CHARLES: *(joining his brother in pushing him out)* Ay, out with him, certainly!

SIR OLIVER: This violence—

JOSEPH: Sir, 'tis your own fault.

CHARLES: Out with him, to be sure. *(They all but shove Sir Oliver into Sir Peter, Lady Teazle, Maria, and Rowley, who enter in a body.)*

SIR PETER: *(in noisy amazement)* My old friend, Sir Oliver; hey! What in the name of wonder! Here are

---

[1] Used as a password for entrance to private societies.

dutiful nephews! Assault their uncle at a first visit!

LADY TEAZLE: Indeed, Sir Oliver, 'twas well we came in to rescue you.

ROWLEY: *(amused)* Truly, it was; for I perceive Sir Oliver, the character of old Stanley was no protection to you.

SIR OLIVER: *(catching his breath)* Nor of Premium either: the necessities of the former could not extort a shilling from that benevolent gentleman *(nodding toward Joseph and then looking sharply at Charles);* and now, egad, I stood a chance of faring worse than my ancestors, and being knocked down without being bid for.

JOSEPH: Charles!

CHARLES: Joseph!

JOSEPH: *(heavily)* 'Tis now complete!

CHARLES: *(gulping)* Very!

SIR OLIVER: *(severely)* Sir Peter, my friend, and Rowley too—look on that elder nephew of mine. You know what he has already received from my bounty; and you also know how gladly I would have regarded half my fortune as held in trust for him. Judge then my disappointment in discovering him to be destitute of faith, charity, and gratitude.

SIR PETER: Sir Oliver, I should be more surprised at this declaration, if I had not myself found him to be mean, treacherous, and hypocritical.

LADY TEAZLE: And if the gentleman pleads not guilty to these, pray let him call *me* to his character.

SIR PETER: Then, I believe, we need add no more. If he knows himself, he will consider it as the most perfect punishment, that he is known to the world.

CHARLES: *(aside)* If they talk this way to honesty, what will they say to me, by and by?

SIR OLIVER: *(with an air of even more complete contempt)* As for that prodigal, his brother, there—

CHARLES: *(aside)* Ay, now comes my turn; the damned family pictures will ruin me!

JOSEPH: *(in a tone of outraged dignity)* Sir Oliver— uncle, will you honor me with a hearing?

CHARLES: *(aside)* Now if Joseph would make one of his long speeches, I might recollect myself a little.

SIR PETER: *(to Joseph)* I suppose you would undertake to justify yourself entirely?

JOSEPH: I trust I could.

SIR OLIVER: *(to Charles)* Well, sir! and you could justify yourself too, I suppose?

CHARLES: *(wryly)* Not that I know of, Sir Oliver.

SIR OLIVER: What! Little Premium has been let too much into the secret, I suppose?

CHARLES: True, sir; but they were *family secrets*, and should not be mentioned again, you know.

ROWLEY: Come, Sir Oliver, I know you cannot speak of Charles's follies with anger.

SIR OLIVER: *(genially dropping his pose of severity)* Odd's heart, no more can I; nor with gravity either. Sir Peter, do you know the rogue bargained with me for all his ancestors; sold me judges and generals by the foot, and maiden aunts as cheap as broken china!

CHARLES: To be sure, Sir Oliver, I did make a little free with the family canvas, that's the truth on't. My ancestors may rise in judgment against me, there's no denying it; but believe me sincere when I tell you—and upon my soul I would not say so if I was not—that if I do not appear mortified at the exposure of my follies, it is because I feel at this moment the warmest satisfaction in seeing you, my liberal benefactor.

SIR OLIVER: *(heartily)* Charles, I believe you! Give me your hand again; the ill-looking little fellow over the settee has made your peace.

CHARLES: Then, sir, my gratitude to the original is still increased.

LADY TEAZLE: *(nodding toward Maria)* Yet I believe, Sir Oliver, here is one whom Charles is still more anxious to be reconciled to.

SIR OLIVER: Oh, I have heard of his attachment there; and, with the young lady's pardon, if I construe right—that blush—

SIR PETER: *(impatiently)* Well, child, speak your sentiments!

MARIA: *(faintly)* Sir, I have little to say, but that I shall rejoice to hear that he is happy; for me—whatever claim I had to his affection, I willingly resign to one who has a better title.

CHARLES: *(not believing his ears)* How, Maria!

SIR PETER: *(baffled)* Hey day! what's the mystery now? While he appeared an incorrigible rake, you would give your hand to no one else; and now that he is likely to reform, I'll warrant you won't have him.

MARIA: *(with clear directness)* His own heart and Lady Sneerwell know the cause!

CHARLES: *(with extreme puzzlement)* Lady Sneerwell!

JOSEPH: *(still in his exalted sententious manner)* Brother, it is with great concern I am obliged to speak on this point, but my regard to justice compels me, and Lady Sneerwell's injuries can no longer be concealed. *(Dramatically, he opens the door to the room where Lady Sneerwell is concealed. She enters with lowered head.)*

SIR PETER: *(aghast)* So! another French milliner! Egad, he has one in every room of the house, I suppose.

LADY SNEERWELL: *(affecting embarrassment and deep sorrow)* Ungrateful Charles! Well may you be surprised, and feel for the indelicate situation your perfidy has forced me into.

CHARLES: *(utterly bewildered)* Pray, uncle, is this another plot of yours? For, as I have life, I don't understand it.

JOSEPH: *(sternly)* I believe, sir, there is but the evidence of one person more necessary to make it extremely clear.

SIR PETER: *(deliberately)* And that person, I imagine, is Mr. Snake. Rowley, you were perfectly right to bring him with us, and pray let him appear.

ROWLEY: *(turning toward the left)* Walk in, Mr. Snake.

(He comes in.) I thought his testimony might be wanted; however, it happens unluckily that he comes to confront Lady Sneerwell, not to support her.

LADY SNEERWELL: *(aside)* Villain! Treacherous to me at last! *(to Snake)* Speak, fellow; have you too conspired against me?

SNAKE: *(glibly)* I beg your ladyship ten thousand pardons; you paid me extremely liberally for the lie in question; but I unfortunately have been offered double to speak the truth.

SIR PETER: Plot and counter-plot, egad!

LADY SNEERWELL: *(enraged)* The torments of shame and disappointment on you all!

LADY TEAZLE: *(evenly)* Hold, Lady Sneerwell! Before you go, let me thank you for the trouble you and that gentleman have taken, in writing letters from me to Charles, and answering them yourself; and let me also request you to make my respects to the scandalous college, of which you are president, and inform them that Lady Teazle, licentiate, begs leave to return the diploma they gave her, as she leaves off practice, and kills characters no longer.

LADY SNEERWELL: *(leaving in a white fury)* You too, madam—provoking—insolent! May your husband live these fifty years! *(She disappears through the wings at the left.)*

SIR PETER: Oons! what a fury!

LADY TEAZLE: A malicious creature, indeed!

SIR PETER: *(picking her up sharply)* Hey, Not for her last wish?

LADY TEAZLE: *(melting)* Oh, no!

SIR OLIVER: *(to Joseph)* Well, sir, and what have you to say now?

JOSEPH: *(hypocritical to the bitter end)* Sir, I am so confounded, to find that Lady Sneerwell could be guilty of suborning Mr. Snake in this manner, to impose on us all, that I know not what to say. *(with broad solicitude)* However, lest her revengeful spirit should prompt her to injure my brother, I had certainly better follow her directly. *(He bows low as if untouched by any of these disclosures, and leaves with dignity.)*

SIR PETER: *(marvelling)* Moral to the last drop!

SIR OLIVER: *(looking after him)* Ay, and marry her, Joseph, if you can. Oil and vinegar, egad! you'll do very well together.

ROWLEY: *(in polite inquiry)* I believe we have no more occasion for Mr. Snake at present?

SNAKE: *(seemingly penitent)* Before I go, I beg pardon once for all, for whatever uneasiness I have been the humble instrument of causing to the parties present.

SIR PETER: *(cordially)* Well, well, you have made atonement by a good deed at last.

SNAKE: But I must request of the company that it shall never be known.

SIR PETER: *(still susceptible to being shocked)* Hey! What the plague! Are you ashamed of having done a right thing once in your life?

SNAKE: *(sighing deeply)* Ah, sir! consider; I live by the badness of my character. I have nothing but my infamy to depend on! and if it were once known that I had been betrayed into an honest action, I should lose every friend I have in the world. *(He turns to go.)*

SIR OLIVER: *(as Snake departs)* Well, well; we'll not traduce you by saying anything in your praise, never fear.

SIR PETER: *(shaking his head)* There's a precious rogue!

LADY TEAZLE: *(calling attention to the fact that Maria has moved over to Charles and taken his hand)* See, Sir Oliver, there needs no persuasion now to reconcile your nephew and Maria.

SIR OLIVER: *(heartily)* Ay, ay, that's as it should be, and egad we'll have the wedding tomorrow morning.

CHARLES: Thank you, dear uncle!

SIR PETER: *(with mock severity)* What, you rogue! don't you ask the girl's consent first?

CHARLES: Oh, I have done that a long time—a minute ago—and she has looked *yes*.

MARIA: *(blushing)* For shame, Charles! I protest, Sir Peter, there has not been a word.

SIR OLIVER: Well, then, the fewer the better. May your love for each other never know abatement.

SIR PETER: And may you live as happily together as Lady Teazle and I intend to do!

CHARLES: *(earnestly)* Rowley, my old friend, I am sure you congratulate me; and I suspect that I owe you much.

SIR OLIVER: You do indeed, Charles.

ROWLEY: *(modestly)* If my efforts to serve you had not succeeded, you would have been in my debt for the attempt; but deserve to be happy, and you overpay me.

SIR PETER: Ay, honest Rowley always said you would reform.

CHARLES: Why, as to reforming, Sir Peter, I'll make no promises, and that I take to be a proof that I intend to set about it; but here shall be my monitor—my gentle guide. Ah! can I leave the virtuous path those eyes illumine? *(turning to Maria with deep sincerity)*

> Though thou, dear maid, shouldst waive thy beauty's sway,
> Thou still must rule, because I will obey:
> An humble fugitive from Folly view,
> No sanctuary near but Love and you.

(opening his arms in a pleading gesture to the audience)

> You can, indeed, each anxious fear remove,
> For even Scandal dies if you approve.

EPILOGUE

by Mr. Colman[1]

Spoken by Lady Teazle

> I, who was late so volatile and gay,
> Like a trade wind must now blow all one way,
> Bend all my cares, my studies, and my vows,

---

[1] George Colman (1732-1794), popular playwright and theatre manager.

To one dull rusty weathercock—my spouse!
So wills our virtuous bard—the motley Bayes[2]
Of crying epilogues and laughing plays!
Old bachelors, who marry smart young wives,
Learn from our play to regulate your lives:
Each bring his dear to town, all faults upon her,
London will prove the very source of honor.
Plunged fairly in, like a cold bath it serves,
When principles relax, to brace the nerves.
Such is my case; and yet I must deplore
That the gay dream of dissipation's o'er.
And say, ye fair, was ever lively wife,
Born with a genius for the highest life,
Like me untimely blasted in her bloom,
Like me condemn'd to such a dismal doom?
Save money—when I just knew how to waste it!
Leave London—just as I began to taste it!
Must I then watch the early crowing cock,
The melancholy ticking of a clock;
In a lone rustic hall forever pounded,[3]
With dogs, cats, rats, and squalling brats surrounded?
With humble curate can I now retire
(While good Sir Peter boozes with the squire),
And at backgammon mortify my soul,
That pants for loo, or flutters at the vole?[4]
Seven's the main![5] Dear sound that must expire,
Lost at hot cockles[6] round a Christmas fire!
The transient hour of fashion too soon spent,
Farewell the tranquil mind, farewell content!
Farewell the plumèd head, the cushioned tête
That takes the cushion from its proper seat![7]

---

[2] Theatrical vernacular name for a playwright.
[3] Imprisoned.
[4] Loo was a card game of the time, vole the equivalent of a slam in bridge.
[5] Lucky number at dice.
[6] A country game, variation of blind man's bluff.
[7] Satiric reference to the gigantic headdresses, as if seat cushions were piled on the head.

The spirit-stirring drum—card drums[8] I mean!
Spadille—odd trick—pam—basto—king and queen![9]
And you, ye knockers, that, with brazen throat,
The welcome visitors' approach denote!
Farewell all quality of high renown,
Pride, pomp, and circumstance of glorious town!
Farewell! your revels I partake no more,
And Lady Teazle's occupation's o'er!
All this I told our bard; he smiled, and said 'twas
    clear,
I ought to play deep tragedy next year.
Meanwhile he drew wise morals from his play,
And in these solemn periods stalk'd away: —
"Blest were the fair like you! her faults who stopp'd,
And closed her follies when the curtain dropp'd!
No more in vice or error to engage,
Or play the fool at large on life's great stage."

---

[8] Card parties.
[9] Current names of valuable cards.

BIBLIOGRAPHY

THE PLAYWRIGHT

W. A. Darlington, *Sheridan*. London: Duckworth, 1933.

Kenelm Foss, *Here Lies Richard Brinsley Sheridan*. London: M. Secker, 1939.

Lewis Gibbs (pseudonym of Joseph Walter Cove), *Sheridan*. London: J. M. Dent, 1947.

Alice Glasgow, *Sheridan of Drury Lane*. New York: Frederick A. Stokes Co., 1940.

Raymond C. Rhodes, *Harlequin Sheridan*. Oxford: B. Blackwell, 1933.

THE PLAY

The Dramatic Works of Richard Brinsley Sheridan, introduction by Joseph Knight. Oxford and New York: Oxford University Press, H. Milford, 1930.

Major Dramas of Richard Brinsley Sheridan, introduction and notes by George Henry Nettleton. Boston and London: Ginn & Co., 1906.

The Plays and Poems of Richard Brinsley Sheridan, edited by R. Crompton Rhodes, 3 vols. Oxford: Basil Blackwood, 1928; New York: The Macmillan Co., 1929.

THE STAGING

Richard Southern, *Changeable Scenery, Its Origin and Development in the English Theatre*. London: Faber and Faber, 1951.